Toxic Loves, Impossible Futures

CRITICAL
MEXICAN STUDIES

Critical Mexican Studies
Series editor: Ignacio M. Sánchez Prado

Critical Mexican Studies is the first English-language, humanities-based, theoretically focused academic series devoted to the study of Mexico. The series is a space for innovative works in the humanities that focus on theoretical analysis, transdisciplinary interventions, and original conceptual framing.

Toxic Loves, Impossible Futures

Feminist Living as Resistance

Irmgard Emmelhainz

Vanderbilt University Press
Nashville, Tennessee

Library of Congress Cataloging-in-Publication Data
Names: Emmelhainz, Irmgard, author.
Title: Toxic loves, impossible futures : feminist living as resistance /
    Irmgard Emmelhainz.
Description: Nashville, Tennessee : Vanderbilt University Press, [2021] |
    Series: Critical Mexican studies | Includes index.
Identifiers: LCCN 2021035784 (print) | LCCN 2021035785 (ebook) | ISBN
    9780826502445 (paperback) | ISBN 9780826502452 (hardcover) | ISBN
    9780826502469 (epub) | ISBN 9780826502476 (pdf)
Subjects: LCSH: Feminism—History—21st century.
Classification: LCC HQ1111 .E46 2021 (print) | LCC HQ1111 (ebook) | DDC
    305.42—dc23

LC record available at https://lccn.loc.gov/2021035784
LC ebook record available at https://lccn.loc.gov/2021035785

Some passages of this book have been taken and expanded from the following:
"Dragging (My) Shadows on a Circle: On Anger, Vulnerability and Intimacy," *e-flux journal #92*, June 2018, available online: https://www.e-flux.com/journal/92/204505/dragging-my-shadows-on-a-circle-on-anger-vulnerability-and-intimacy.
"Shattering and Healing," *e-flux journal #96*, January 2019, available online: https://www.e-flux.com/journal/96/244461/shattering-and-healing.
"Decolonial Love," *e-flux journal #99*, April 2019, available online: https://www.e-flux.com/journal/99/262398/decolonial-love.

To Lizzy and Layla. Roberta too.

Contents

Introduction

My hands itch to write
imposed idleness
now heal!
For it all must flood out
ten fingers dancing
sprinkling
in full speed
on the keyboard
or I might drown
soon
on unarticulated thoughts . . .
Irmgard Emmelhainz

I was born resisting, I bloomed from the cracks, I held onto life with the roots I managed to
weave through the pavement opening up paths to find my own nourishment.
"The Coyote Woman" from *Historias propias desde casa* **by Lorena Wolffer**

The fact that the glaciers are melting is seemingly abstract to us as is the
news that the Amazon Forest is burning up at the speed of an entire foot-
ball stadium per minute. Yet, breathing in Mexico City feels indeed like the
Apocalypse; the interdependent fabric that sustains life on earth, including
human life, is tirelessly being torn up by market forces; the barriers between
humans and machines seem to blur, making humans obsolete, especially
our faculty of reason; culture has become entertainment and algorithms;
constantly, we are invited to achieve a state of bliss by cultivating our feelings, to save ourselves with self-love, to seek sexual gratification, and to liberate ourselves from the obligations of social and family life. Yet we have
completely lost our sense of belonging. We foresee a future in which most
of humanity will be redundant, and an answer to the double challenge of

globalization and global warming seems to be toxic nationalism: the evangelists of the new populism have transformed classism and racism into rhetorical weapons that have polarized society and destroyed the public sphere by replacing reasonable dialogue with passionate shit storms. Meanwhile, atavistic essentialisms have been unearthed to build a new version of the "Fatherland" based on a moral struggle against corruption, "foreign" interests, and power in our territory, all legitimating the schizophrenia displayed by the ruler. In the meantime, a war is being waged against those defending their territories and against leaders of movements against environmental devastation. "Narco" violence intensifies while the poor are given cash bonuses, knowing that they will not have a place in the system in the short or long term.

Disinformation campaigns in social media modulate our moods, establishing frames for false debates fragmenting political imagination.

What is the task of thought and reflection before this landscape? The role of writing (*écriture*) in a world of refugees, people living in situations of survival, in which writing has been put at the service of the culture industry to entertain the privileged classes, with the burden of performing superficial gestures of inclusion and democracy, is currently unclear. In a country in which most people live by the day, idiosyncrasy passes for reflection while confession—the privileged form of women's self-expression—proliferates in social media besieged by narcissism, affect, and private emotionality made public. What does it mean today to be a writer, when disinformation and propaganda reach the degree zero of the world? What is the place of intellectuals in a worldless and wordless place, as polysemy has been stolen, the meaning of words distorted, language expropriated from its quality of being a *true* descriptor of reality by power?

According to Arundhati Roy, writers and readers build the site of writing together, a site that is extremely fragile yet indestructible because it is ceaselessly built like a refuge. *Écriture* is like a trench that allows us to peep, dodge, and counterattack an invisible enemy that is penetrating and overwhelming, working us from within. Clearly our present world is making an urgent call to intrinsically tie politics and writing, especially in a country in which violence traverses the pores of all bodies, obliterating spaces of enunciation and living-together, while a rhetoric of freedom of expression prevails as merchandise that co-exists unproblematically with the ubiquity of State violence. Writing is a refuge and a trench to resist the closure of spaces for conspiring, writing stories, discussing, proposing alternatives, designing utopias, to collectively do reproductive labor, to expose ideas, to resist against the threat of the imposition of a certain "should be" of culture and cultural politics. The problem that concerns us writers, which we clearly share with activists and others dedicated to creation, is finding a balance between creativity and critical thinking, negativity and opposing consciousness. From a situated feminist position, acknowledging the intersectionality of feminist struggles, always asking self-reflexively, Where am I speaking from? About whom and how?

We need to find strategies to maintain open relationships between ideas and practice, theory and activism, while being conscious that one does not necessarily precede the other. Specifically, writing can help us think through means to resist the present, violence, the vulgarity of our times, and to express our anger and be worthy of our epoch, engaging with the present in an oppositional and productive way.

In this collection of essays I establish dialogue with imaginary and real friends like bell hooks, Sarah Ahmed, Leslie Jamison, Lina Meruane, Leanne Simpson, Chris Kraus, Alaíde Foppa, Lorena Wolffer, Sayak Valencia, Pip Day, Veronica González, Eimear McBride, Simone de Beauvoir, Elena Poniatowska, Susan Lauren Berlant, Margaret Randall, Arundhati Roy, Marta Lamas, Dawn Paley, Verónica Gago, Simone Weil, Naomi Klein, and others.

These reflections incorporate their voices in an urgent attempt to resist the present in their company, in a world in which "a woman's voice" exists in bodies called on to occupy important positions in corporations, government, cultural and academic institutions, to work in factories, to join the army, but whose bodies are systematically rendered vulnerable by gender violence and by the double burden imposed on us to perform both productive and reproductive labor. I am summoning these writers to help me think up systems to undo misogynist social practices and to disarticulate patriarchy's submission and denigration tricks against women, elaborating a genealogy of feminist gazes and voices to help me become stronger, more rooted. To envision the urgent cognitive shift to collectively tumble-down heteropatriarchy. And from there on, to draw a map of our current political-environmental problems and conceive a point of departure to resist together. In these texts, "a woman's voice" parts from issues of gender, female sexuality, and pain to encompass modernism and capitalism, to discussions of art, film, and literature, to the pitfalls of Leftist thinking before our current crisis of uprooting and alienation, COVID-19, massive violence and environmental crisis and how they are interlinked, enabled by the denigration of life and human relationships. Indeed, gender and environmental violence originate in the same epistemological site. This "woman's voice" also addresses class and race tensions, solidarity, empathy, happiness, despotic empathy, addiction, and codependency crossing through the Palestine Question, State violence, and the Neoliberal War currently being waged in Mexico against the redundant populations.

This book is written for Layla García thanks to complicities shared with Pip Day, Julieta Aranda, Silvia Gruner, Lizzy Cancino, Gabriela Rangel, Karen Cordero, Michelle Sanz, Margaret Schlubach, my FEM students, Lina Meruane, María Virginia Jaua, Ignacio Sánchez Prado, María José Bruña, Lorena Wolffer, Miguel Ventura, Isabel Vericat, Lorena Glinz, Helga Kaiser, Silvia Gruner, Eshrat Erfanian, and Sara Eliassen. It originated in conversations with Pip Day while doing a residency in Montréal hosted by OBORO and the SBC Gallery that led to our co-curated exhibition *Does the Oyster Sleep?* The exhibition was reiterated at the TPW Gallery in Toronto in 2017. Versions of essays commissioned by Julieta Aranda for a special *e-flux journal* issue on feminism appear. The book, originally in Spanish, was written thanks to a grant by the Fondo Nacional para la Cultura y las Artes (FONCA or Mexican National Fund for Culture and the Arts 2018–2020).

J'ai une voix de ce qu'on appelle "femme"

Apostrophe is not only the condition of love but an ideal of self-encounter. For the addressee, you are willing to make provisional clarities. For the addressee, you are willing to perform an openness that's an optimistic brokenness. If you're lucky, you're a topos in your own world, although without the apostrophic phantom you cannot exist in the world . . . if language could pull it off . . . that is the hope of love.

Lauren Berlant[1]

La lutte des femmes sera collective ou elle ne sera pas; il ne s'agît pas seulement d'être libre.

Agnès Varda in "Les plages d'Agnès" (2008)

When standing in line outside a packed public bathroom assigned to women, I always wonder, What are architects thinking when they unfailingly build an equal number of toilet stalls for both men and women, when it is a proven fact that women need to use the bathroom much more often than men? I usually fight the urge to relieve myself and the temptation to dash out to the men's restroom by foreseeing the likely embarrassing event of running into a male user of the space. Because in truth, I no longer feel like I need to make a statement about my own gender (or sex?!). Clearly, our bodies do ground our experience in and of the world and bear both what we call sex *and* what we know as gender. This distinction was conceived to explain biological difference in relationship to social interpretations of that difference. But it seems to me that this distinction fails to explain why, in spite of, or maybe because of women's struggle for equality, architects everywhere keep overlooking that women simply need to use the restroom more often than men. Perhaps it is because feminists, starting with Simone de Beauvoir, were only considering the *reproductive* aspects of the female body as that which makes us different than men, leaving other biological aspects on the side. Evidently the concerns and realities of trans bodies, elderly bodies, or surgically changed bodies are nowhere near this picture of pinning down difference in terms of biological needs. For early twentieth-century feminists, the source of female oppression was the fact that women had been historically defined by their bodies. For de Beauvoir, the ontological existence of females is specifically rooted in the need for human reproduction, and that confines woman to her own sex:[2] a *woman* is a uterus, an ovary, she is *female* and that word is enough to define her. But this is why de Beauvoir posited female bodies as alienated and opaque, the alienation being exacerbated by pregnancy and by the exhausting servitude of breastfeeding, among other things. When women reach menopause, according to de Beauvoir, they can escape the servitudes of the female and become free from the yoke of reproduction and be consistent with themselves, perhaps forming a "third sex."[3] In comparison, "man's genital life does not thwart his personal existence" like it does the existence of women. Countering Sigmund Freud's anathema indictment that "anatomy is destiny," de Beauvoir was therefore the first feminist to draw a distinction between species (biology, sex) and society: for her, the species realizes its existence in a society, and therefore a woman's body is by no means enough to define her, and thus *one is not born a woman but becomes a woman*. From a feminist point of view, therefore, society's customs cannot be reduced to biology, because biology cannot solely provide an answer to the question of woman's oppression. This is why the battle of twentieth-century feminism to liberate women was first of all a struggle to free her from the physical constraints of reproduction.

The matter of the bodily liberation of women was at the center of my friends Jimena Acosta and Michelle Millar Fisher's exhibition *I Will What I Want: Women, Design and Empowerment*.[4] I went with Acosta to see the show, which gathers objects designed to alleviate woman's bodily reproductive burden by enabling her to take control her own fertility, fluids, and reproductive process: the internal condom, dial pill dispenser, sanitary pads, ruby cup, upright birthing chair, breast pump, baby carrier, gender-neutral toys, et cetera. It struck us that the exhibition posits design's complex and contradictory role in gender expression and equality, and the fact that the material world is largely designed by and for men, but consumed also by those who identify as women. *I Will What I Want* is a collection of manufactured objects that have sought to positively shape female experiences and to help women emancipate themselves. At the same time, it underscores how not only the reproductive function but also biological information are essential elements to women's (and to men's) experience in the world. The pressing issue of the meaning of the female body as a natural fact is brought up in the juxtaposition of objects designed to alleviate menstruation with photographs by Arvida Byström that depict women in everyday situations whose menstruation transpires uncontrolled through their clothes, and with a reproduction of the viral image of Kiran Gandhi, who ran the London Marathon in August 2015 menstruating without protection. I think that Byström's photographs and Gandhi's gesture radically bring into question the consideration of the body as a merely cultural situation separate from biological facts, and the definition of "feminist" as a female who needs to detach herself from her bodily functions in order to join the ranks of egalitarian humanity. And that perhaps it is necessary to rethink the gender/sex distinction, which has been premised on, I suspect, the mind/body separation upon which Western epistemology has been built.

According to Judith Butler, because women were historically identified with their anatomy, and this identification served to oppress us, de Beauvoir gave feminists the task to identify themselves with "consciousness." That is to say, women's emancipation meant to enact transcendental activity that would not restricted by the body. In the Western differentiation between "men" and "women," the latter, as we have seen, had been defined by corporeality, as "biologically determined," and the latter were conceived as enabled to transcend their bodies toward "reason," become a meta-consciousness.[5] And I pondered on the fact that the sex/gender division not only follows the Western mind/body split, but obeys the feminist need to liberate women from their enslaving bodies so that they can transcend their corporeal status and become "consciousness," like men. This is why we have insisted on the body as a *situation*: as the site for cultural interpretations, a material reality defined by a social context. And herein lies the paradox laid out by the collection of objects exhibited in *I Will What I Want*: is emancipatory design actually grounded on immanent bodily needs, or are the objects designed interpretations of those needs tied to the specific feminist concern to undo anatomical difference to achieve gender equality?

Then I realized that to think about biology as determinant of women's experience, as it is aligned with the nature/culture dichotomy, is to think about coercion. And it is precisely the objects in *I Will What I Want* that enabled women to enter the productive workforce in the 1970s, by enabling control of / erasing / palliating the reproductive function. This is highlighted by the juxtaposition in the exhibition between "Finding Her" posters by DDB Dubai for the UN, and a display of an array of breast pumps. In a way, the juxtaposition between the breast pumps and the posters designed in 2017 (focusing on three particularly male-dominated industries: politics, science, and technology) to draw attention to the lack of women in the Egyptian workforce, which is only 23 percent female, opposes the feminist assertion that biology is not necessary for women's politics. For instance, following de Beauvoir, Gayle Rubin dissociated the study of gender from the study of sexuality in the 1970s. In her view, biological explanations are unlinked to the political because sex and sexuality are natural forms previous to social life: "The body, genitals and capacity for language are necessary components of human sexuality; but they do not determine its content, its experience nor its institutional forms."[6] Sex is understood as penis, vagina, testicles, estrogen, and they all have nothing to do with politics. Gender is, according to this account, "everything else," that is, a system of social signification and semiotic formation.

Taking a different stand than Rubin, Judith Butler read Simone de Beauvoir's axiom "one is not born a woman, but one becomes a woman" not as a call to alleviate the female reproductive function, but as a battle for *gender*. For Butler, gender is an identity that both precedes the self at birth and is gradually acquired. But for Butler, while sex is an invariant factual aspect of the body, what concerns feminism is the *acculturation* of that body. The distinction between sex and gender serves to attribute the value of the social functions of women to biological necessity, and to cease to refer credibly to gendered behavior as "natural" or "nonnatural." For Butler, all gender is "nonnatural" and the feminist project is to underscore the presumption between a causal or mimetic relation between sex and gender. That is to say, "becoming a woman" is a subjective, cultural interpretation of being female that is completely independent of the ontological condition of "being female."[7] While bodies are "natural," genders are "constructed," and "being female" and "being a woman" are two different kinds of being. Therefore, gender is a process of self-construction that implies assuming certain corporeal style and its meaning, and thus *gender is inscribed in the biological body* (conceived as a passive medium). In other words, "becoming" a gender is a choice and acculturation and implies subjecting oneself to a cultural situation as well as creating one. For Butler, it is not that the body needs to be liberated from the reproductive function, but rather, from oppressive social interpretations of the reproductive body.

But somewhat, to be able to construct one's gender still feels like a trap. Maybe there can be more answers if we rethink the relationship between "me" and "my sex organs" and the rest of my biological information, if we incorporate biology into how we think our bodies, aside from them being blank slates in which cultural norms and non-normative gender mean-ings can be rejected and reinscribed. I started thinking about this when my partner began having hormonal fluctuations and still doctors have not been able to sort her out because the lab studies had always come out "aver-age" to them. A passage about family and gender in Maggie Nelson's *The Argonauts* brings forth in part what I'm trying to get at: that maybe bodies are not empty vessels with biological functions detachable from a cultural function. Because although we actually reappropriate gender and inscribe it on our own bodies in our own terms and we have re-invented kinship rela-tions, there is some kind of trap we always fail to get out of. In that passage, Nelson tells the story about how a friend came over to her house and got a mug for coffee that had been given to Nelson by her mother. The mug has a photo of Nelson's family all dressed up to go to the *Nutcracker* at Christ-mastime—a ritual, she tells us, she enjoyed with her mother when she was little and that she revived with her own family. When seeing the mug, her friend exclaimed, "I have never seen anything so heteronormative in all my life."[8] But what is heteronormative about the photograph? Nelson ponders:

> That my mother made a mug on a boojie service like Snapfish? That we're clearly participating, or acquiescing into participating, in a long tradition of families being photographed at holiday time in their holiday best? That my mother made me the mug, in part to indicate that she recognizes and accepts my tribe as family? What about my pregnancy—is that inherently hetero-normative? Or is it the presumed opposition of queerness and procreation (or, to put a finer edge on it, maternity) more a reactionary embrace of how things have shaken down for queers than the mark of some ontological truth?[9]

Is it about queers having children? Is heteronormativity linked to the "female animal"? Although we have learned to exist in our bodies by recon-figuring given gender norms, I, too, like Nelson, feel trapped. We thought that emancipation meant that we could dissociate ourselves from our own reproduction function—or to choose it over an array of other gender pos-sibilities. But maybe the problem I am trying to articulate resides in, on the one hand, the inferior role of biology in the way we think of ourselves as "culturally constructed entities" and, on the other, the way the status of reproduction in neoliberal Western societies has been undermined by capitalism and by the feminist battle for liberation from the reproductive function. And as a result, we are undergoing what Nancy Fraser has called a "crisis of care." She explains how women who give birth still have pressure to nourish and educate children, look after friends and family members, to

FIGURE 1. Layla's birthday (2017), photo courtesy of the author.

keep up homes and communities, and in general, to sustain connections.[10] These "social reproduction" processes—affective and material labor without pay—are indispensable for capitalist societies. Without reproductive labor there would be no culture, no economy, no political organization. (We would have no food in the fridge or on the table, no clean clothes; conflicted as I am on this matter, I am grateful we can have someone to help us out with domestic labor.)

And yet reproductive labor has been systematically disregarded and invisi-bilized; it is neither remunerated nor recognized, and it is still being imposed on women because someone needs to do it and because it has been proven that a society that systematically undermines social reproduction cannot last for very long. A case in question can be the social implosion and spiral of violence that predates Mexican cities like Tijuana and Ciudad Juárez, where women have joined the workforce as sweatshop workers. Lacking a social, corporate, or familial network of support care, their children have turned to criminal activities as early as the teenage years. For Fraser, the crisis of reproduction also manifests globally and it encompasses economic, ecologi-cal, and political aspects that intersect and exacerbate one another. Care is sacrificed, and in general, the ways we are sustaining life itself have been impoverished for the sake of the sustained accumulation of capital. Just as women have needed to dissociate their bodies from their reproductive func-tion to be free from the yoke of sexual difference, capitalist societies have separated social reproduction from economic production, associating the first with women and considering it low value. While the "domestic sphere" is obscured and rendered irrelevant, the work of giving birth and socializ-ing children is central to capitalism, as is looking after the elderly, keeping up homes, building communities, and sustaining shared meanings.[11] And yet the value of reproduction is rejected both by feminists and by capital-ism. Women who have joined the productive workforce need to subcontract family and community care. In this new organization of social reproduction, care has become merchandise for those who can afford it. Leïla Slimani's novel *Chanson douce* (2016) addresses the commodity status of reproduc-tion and the tensions it raises between personal life and affective entangle-ments.[12] The premise of Slimani's Goncourt prize–winning novel (she is the second Moroccan and twelfth woman to have been awarded it) is the mur-dering of two children by the nanny who looks after them. She thus draws a primal scene of care exchange value, which costs anxieties, hypocrisies, and inequalities, all arising from the logic of care itself, which covers power and exploitation relationships. In our globalized world, privileged women have to pay—sometimes a significant percentage of their salary—for the right to join the ranks of productive labor. As women are considered equal as men in all spheres, we look out for the equal opportunities we deserve to realize our talents in the sphere of production. Reproduction, therefore, becomes an uncomfortable residue, a costly obstacle for advancement and for the liberation of women.

Some conclusions I'm drawing from all of this are that while culture does play a broad role in giving shape to differences among genders, denying the role of reproduction in society, which is the same as denying the role of biology in our lives (to the extreme of Soylent, Excedrin, and other neoliberal excesses to maximize productivity, even the Silicon Valley fantasy of downloading the self onto the virtual sphere completely), has proven to be both dangerous and a trap that keeps a significant portion of women's ordeals in the darkness. In *Gut Feminism*, Elizabeth Wilson proposes incorporating biological information to rethink mental and corporeal states in relationship to gender.[13] That is to say, to consider the body beyond the way it has been described by culture or inscribed into cultural contexts, as shaped by biology. For instance, if cultural constructivism determines that men behave aggressively not because of testosterone but because of "toxic masculinities," perhaps Paul B. Preciados' experiments with testosterone are a much needed empirical and conceptual bridge between biological bodies and cultural interpretations of them.[14] Also Preciado's concept of the "pharmacopornographic regime" (inspired by Monique Wittig's materialist analysis of female oppression and precedented by Foucault's disciplinary regime) is key to understanding how we experience sex, gender, and sexuality as determined by two of the biggest industries of the twentieth century: pharmaceutics and pornography. That is to say, according to Preciado, science, visual culture, and capitalism have a role to play in how we live gender. In the 1950s, he argues, key events modified radically the administration of bodies, establishing a model of synthetic control that operates almost invisibly from within the body, at the molecular level, modifying directly the chemical composition of individuals. First, the event of the separation of the reproductive function from sexuality, enabled by the availability of the contraception pill, opened up the way for the scientific fabrication of femininity. Through synthetic hormones, the pill executes a double operation that cuts menstruation to artificially restitute it. In other words, hormonal hyper sensibilization is chemically induced by a pharmaceutic transnational. This means for Preciado that "feminine" biological truth is neither a natural circumstance nor an immutable reality, but manipulable by the pill: a kind of an ingestible Panopticon. Second, the pornographic image has been the most effective apparatus to transform representation into matter. This means that through the pornographic depiction of bodies and desire, sexuality has been radically transformed into permanent stimulation and excitement without achieving pleasure. Together, the pill and pornography have enabled new forms of dominance and submission to a heterosexual, white political and cultural model of normalization and control.

If cultural constructivism argues that women are more prone to caring and raising children do so because they have been conditioned by the heteropatriarchal order to do it, maybe we should consider transsexuals' need to equate sexual identity with the gonad tissue and genitals or transgender people's contradiction between gender identity and lived experience as evidence that the biological, hormonal, and neurological differences that give shape to gender need to be brought to the table. Because I find it terrifying that the root of the sex/gender divide harks back to the modern conception of man as "reason." Fully dissociated from the body, the ideal condition of "man" translates to the ideal of woman as pure consciousness. If we speak of situated knowledges against universalizing scientific, Eurocentric, and masculine vision, could we embrace a kind of situated biology that would consider not only two or three sexes, but a myriad of sexes that could be expressed limitlessly through our bodies? And from what standpoint could we organize a political struggle that would have as an end a society that would celebrate, support, and value reproduction instead of negating it and undermining it?

Reasonable Murder

The female body is a threat to all rational order because it has been construed as incapable of controlling its own fluids, liquids, viscosities, and secretions. The female body not only lacks a phallus, but and above all, lacks physical and mental self-containment (I am hearing the loud and accusatory voice of my former co-creator in a project as I decided to move on from working together in the presence of a lawyer: "You are [Stop!] being E-MO-TIONAL"). The challenge of feminism is not to deal with these alleged forms of lack of control, but to reject all social structures that objectify our bodies, which includes subjectivation by being subjected through rape and murder.

According to Françoise Héritier, the human species is the only one in the whole planet in which the males allow themselves to murder the females of their species. There are animals that kill nursing or young offspring to put down a rival, making the females fertile again and enabling the murdering male to transmit his own genes. Knowing this, Héritier establishes without hesitating that aggressive human male behavior against females is not an effect of human nature but of the human capacity to reason. This means that humans have somehow built a rational system that legitimates violence against and murder of females. Animals do not murder females because it goes against their own evolution and survival possibilities: females are the only ones capable of reproducing both sexes with their bodies. Differently, humans justify that men rape, hit, or kill the women they believe are at their disposal because of "their masculine nature." But this is plain wrong. Men rape, hit, or kill women because of "reason" and "culture."[1] This is why our challenge is to become embodied differently than in heteropatriarchal subjection, in which "becoming woman" means to embody specific forms of submission to power. That is to say, under heteropatriarchy, gender is introduced forcefully into the body. "To become a woman" results from a violent social relation; "woman" is a political and ideological formation based on the constitutive negation that women are raped, exploited, and murdered.[2] Violence is necessary to preserve the status of the "she-other" as "other." This is why, along with embodying ourselves beyond gender, we have to destroy what is known as "the individual."

A Sensorium of Violence

In her brilliant book *Gore Capitalism*, Sayak Valencia explains contemporary forms of explicit violence, describing the capitalist predatory uses of bodies as a form of "necro-empowerment." On the one hand, bodies and human lives are being conceived as merchandise subject to specialized techniques of extreme violence tied to the commerce of murder.[1] Sayak describes how this results in a *gore reality* in which violence is used as a technology of control, a political instrument, and a commodity within the global economy. This reality is constructed through the spectacularization of violence, spreading it out to all fields of knowledge and action. Under *Gore Capitalism*, violence becomes a model for interpreting reality: an *episteme*, in Foucault's sense. On the other hand, Sayak links the unfolding of violence to gender constructions active in Mexico and explains gender violence as exercised by *machos* who, reckoning with their lost honor—because they are poor and threatened by women's incipient emancipation and entry into the productive workforce—use violence to gain riches quickly and to recuperate their lost masculinity, social standing, and territory. In her account, in our gore country, the uses of violence rooted in both the history of State technologies to discipline the body and in heteropatriarchy are now available as a niche merchandise. At the core of gore capitalism is, moreover, a ranking of bodies and lives according to class and gender stratifications that have led to the implosion of civil society through the intensification of violence against poor women and youth. After all, the term *femicide* was coined in Mexico in the 1990s, while the country became a vanguardist laboratory for neoliberal global policies.

Valencia's description of gore capitalism definitely uncovers a mode of systemic violence that is beyond both Walter Benjamin's description of violence in relation to the law, justice, and the Revolution and Slavoj Zizek's distinction between objective violence (which is faceless and abstract) and subjective violence (with a face, like terrorism or crime).[2] Under gore capitalism, for Sayak, violence is an *episteme*—or a *sensorium of violence*, as I would put it—patterns of aggression that mediate social forces and become the matrix of the scene of sociality. In as far as the sensorium of violence shapes gender, race, and class relations, I think that the kind of violence we are discussing here is related to Frantz Fanon's definition of colonial violence.[3] For Fanon, colonial violence gives form to subjectivities and social relations in a double movement of subjection and subjectification propelled by power relations determined by race and gender. In this regard, I would like to posit violence as subtle and not so subtle forms of coercion and abuse that are like an invisible tumor that connects women and minorities. This is rooted in the fact that under heteropatriarchy men behave as if they own the land of originary peoples and also the bodies of the women of their families, while they treat every female body—except for some bodies liberated by taboos—as always potentially penetrable and a source of pleasure.

This shameful situation is the source of internal anger that causes forms of aggression that spread into the social sensorium in different ways. For instance, making women vulnerable to forcefully becoming deposits of silenced male pain can lead them to take out this anger raising their children. I can sense violence everywhere in the landscape, inside everyone, and passing through everything. To me, violence as it is expressed in drug cartel wars, in bullying in elementary schools, in neighbor hostility, at home, in massive species extinctions follows the same logic. Because our Western capitalist societies as a whole are, in essence, predatory. The predatory violence gets into women's bodies sometimes through forms of emotional abuse, which condition women to other forms of abuse, for instance, sexual. In Eimear McBride's extraordinary novel *A Girl Is a Half-Formed Thing* (2014), the author tells the story of a girl who was raised in Catholic Ireland and who, at thirteen, is seduced/raped by one of her uncles. In the passage describing the rape, she records her ambivalence, impotence, disgust, and guilt, but also desire, curiosity, and pain:

Stop stop it you are I don't want.
    Spread fucking open up you sick fucking stupid bitch want the fuck you just like this
    No. Get off.
    They're off fuck knickers off. Thighs in claws I vice. Rip m open. Don't break me open face open. Crushing I hear boines on done he up me fuck

me. Done fuk me open he dine done on me. Done done Til he hye happy
fucky shoves upo comes ui. Kom shitting ut h mith fking kmg
    I'm fking cmin up you.
    Retch I. Retch I. [. . .]
    There bitch there bithc there there
    Stranlge me strangle[4]

The novel is a language experiment reminiscent of Beckett through which
the writer attempts to register visceral sensations that are not yet or near
articulable in words and sentences. The sensorium of violence in *A Girl Is
a Half-Formed Thing* originates in childhood, serving the purpose of what
Rita Segato calls "pedagogy of cruelty," the inscription of gender in female
bodies.[5] But this violence, we know, is not inscribed only in women, but
also in racialized peoples' bodies.

Michel Haneke's films—where the colonial unconscious surfaces as the
unheimlich, for instance in *Caché* (2005) or *Happy End* (2017)—and Michel
Franco's films—like *After Lucía* (2012), about a middle-class teenager whose
bullying by classmates is only brought to the attention of adults around her
when she mysteriously disappears—give us a glimpse of this sensorium of
violence I am trying to describe and how it not only affects all social and
environmental relations in irreversible ways but is brewing inside of us.

But because female anger is never welcome, this sensorium of violence
gives rise to the guilty feeling that we need to contain or modulate our own
capacity for destruction. Personally, I need to find ways not to hurt others
or myself all the time, or invent strategies to channel my internal aggression. Sometimes I'm good at it, other times, I fuck up and rampage against
those whom I love the most or even against total strangers. Other times
I realize that I have become insensitive to some of the things that used to
detonate my internal violence. Because I'm angry and the world is fucked
up, once when I was standing outside of Monsanto's Mexico City corporate
headquarters in Santa Fe, the only thing I could think about was how badly
I wanted to be like Ulrich Meinhof and Valerie Solanas and Leila Khaled
and bomb the shit out of the building. Other times I have fantasies about
destroying supermarkets, banks, corporate headquarters, museums—in
sum, all the places privileged, unknowing, and uncaring heteronormative
assholes circulate. In a world in which violence is ubiquitous and is both
internalized and spread within a sensible landscape of violence, destruction
indeed becomes a means of self-assertion against subjection. In our still-
colonial society, subjectivities are grief-stricken and thus charged with vio-

lence, because when systemic or subjective violence is tolerated and undergone, we feel the need to act it out and spread it unaware.

The general embrace of violence in our still-colonial society is also due to the fact that its legitimacy is grounded on the ongoing erasure of other forms of existence because we have naturalized our predator culture ways. It seems to me that the unconscious force of capitalism is colonialism itself, in the sense of its drive to destroy life and lives for a higher purpose: progress, modernization, universality. One of the consequences of this is the current crisis of relationality and the epidemics of self-destruction.

Expressionist Postcard

To celebrate but not till we pass out—there are children present. Let the party go on until our stomachs hurt from laughing and our feet from dancing. The stand-up comedians had been hired to make jokes and laugh at the guests. "Stand-uping" was the measure of the relationships between the guests and a test of their loyalty to the host in their capacity to laugh at themselves and others, bullying, letting others bully them. The only dark-skinned comedian was making fun of his condition of urbanized Indian and of his stigmatizing by others as "black." To my politically correct sensibility's relief brewed in Canada, the rich African American guests arrived after the dark comedian had ended his routine. Representatives of the middle class catapulted to the 1 percent gathered in a beautiful thirty-bedroom house were being looked after by an equal number of employees, all wearing uniforms with matching shirts bearing the logo of the property and shoes visibly more expensive than the pair I was wearing. We better laugh as the world falls apart, we better have fun and appear like characters in a George Grosz painting, just before or during the catastrophe. I wonder if to an outside observer we seemed grotesque, watching the stand-up comedy show staged on the ecocide. A view of the dam-lake guarded from the horror by our own laughter and by the beautiful sunset only a few could enjoy, the tree canopies drowned on the lake, their tops barely sticking out to laugh with us, trying not to make conscious the slight but inescapable smell of rot and death.

Love Revolution Fear Strike

but it suffices
to set in motion
all of this.
Alaíde Foppa, "El corazón"[1]

Great social movements for freedom and justice have promoted an ethics of love. This implies a concern with the common good of a nation, city, or community grounded on values that nourish and protect well-being. To act on the basis of common good is to assume that our lives and destinies are intimately connected to those of all human and nonhuman inhabitants of the planet. This ethics goes against the root of colonialism: predation, violence, forced displacement, alienation, and detachment. Also against the basis of the capitalist system, which is the deification of separation, personal gain, the instrumentalization of nature, predation as a means to assure the continuity of life, and the mercantilization of the basic structures of interdependence that grant the continuity of (collective and individual) life.

In our society, people live motivated by mass suggestion; everything and everyone is dedicated to producing and consuming more and more; a technocratic bureaucracy and professional politicians govern us, making decisions and executing policies that deny the interdependence of the human and nonhuman worlds. All relationships to other humans and nonhumans now forcibly pass through the market. Our colonial/capitalist society is thus completely antagonistic to love, including contemporary fundamentalist practices of religion, grounded on the negation of the other and thus of the love that is at the heart of all religious traditions.

Communist struggles in Latin America at the second half of the twentieth century (and all over the world) were inspired by a completely different
understanding of interdependence and capitalism than today. Revolutionary militants fought on behalf of a future in which peasants and workers
could be the propellant of their own emancipation from underdevelop-
ment and from their condition as subalterns or colonized, that is, from
their "Third World" status. Two of the revolutionaries' base preoccupations
were the colonial dispossession of Indigenous peoples and the expansion
of the capitalist US Empire. In order to repair the damage and incorporate "the people" in the project of modernity, the goal of Leftist militantism
was to impose a kind of State socialism through armed struggle to achieve
modernity for all. As always in the history of Latin America, a role, a function, and needs were imposed on Indigenous populations that departed
toward a Western and Orientalizing version of their destiny. Carlos Rangel
describes a discursive mutation in the conception of Indigenous peoples
as a move from "the good savage" to being the "good revolutionary" using
cultural or technological European instruments (such as film and photography, social sciences) in order to achieve the revolutionary ideal imposed
upon them. Put to the service of a good cause—their own emancipation—
these instruments implied a paradox of a renewed wave of cultural penetration in Latin America.[2] Later on, I will elucidate the stakes of the de-
Westernization of emancipation struggles of Indigenous peoples—what is
known as "decolonization." What interests me here, however, is the point
of departure of armed struggle in the second half of the twentieth century:
the acknowledgment of a collective destiny shared by all Latin American
criollo, mestizo, and originary populations (peasants and workers). Instead
of considering Indigenous peoples as a world apart, as victims of inequality,
as a threat, as a cheap labor reserve, or as deterritorialized bodies to feed
the necrocapitalist machinery, the interdependence of the Indigenous and
non-Indigenous populations was acknowledged. Above all, after centuries
of abuse and dispossession, what was sought was inclusion for originary
peoples into the Nation-State's modernization project.

For that purpose, at the peak of the Cold War, Leftist militants in Latin
America threw their bodies onto the struggle, putting their lives, skills, and
economic resources at the service of the revolutionary cause with the purpose of changing the social reality of their countries in an organized manner.
This generation of Latin American revolutionaries rebelled against authoritarian, corrupt, and violent regimes, as well as against an economic system
that reproduced misery, ignorance, and violence. For instance, Guatemalan
militants Yolanda Colom and Aura Marina Arriola belonged to a genera-

tion of young people who gave their lives to defend their ideals, taking up arms and embracing the guerrilla. The price was giving up their social status, university titles, family lives, and material wealth, but also physical and mental deterioration due to violence and psychic and material rigor. For the poet, translator, academic, and editor as well as founder of *fem* magazine (who was also from Guatemala but based in Mexico City), Alaíde Foppa (and for many many more), the cost of radicalization was forced disappearance and death.

In her memoirs, brilliant guerrillera and theoretician Aura Marina Arriola offers valuable reflections about the mistakes and successes of Leftists' struggles in Latin America. She recounts that as a young woman, she lived in rural communities in the Guatemalan countryside and that the circumstances she experienced there imposed guerrilla fighting on her, eventually leading her to join the FAR (Fuerzas Armadas Rebeldes or Armed Rebel Forces). As part of the communist elite around Fidel Castro, she lived in Cuba with her partner between 1965 and 1967. Fidel's entourage included Venezuelan militant Elisabeth Burgos and her husband Régis Debray. Along with other *crème de la crème* communists, they lived in privileged circumstances, which Arriola qualifies as "a vice of the revolution."

Arriola participated as actor in the struggle in the historical task of the revolution, as a theoretician and counselor of armed leaders. She was visionary for proposing the formation of bilingual Indigenous leader cadres to incorporate the greatest number possible of Indigenous peoples into the fight. Tireless as she was, while in exile in Rome in 1979, she founded the first solidarity committee with Guatemala, the Delegation of the Democratic Front against Repression. Both Arriola and Yolanda Colom wrote memoirs where they registered the pain and suffering derived from their experiences in the movement: fear, insecurity, misogyny, exile, treason, fall-outs, prosecution, mental and physical ailments.[3] Both women, however, consider the personal damage caused by their political militancy as collateral damage, a necessary sacrifice for the struggle. Self-critiquing her own militancy, Arriola denounces the lapidary attitude of her comrades when they would decide to administer civil death to anyone veering from the cause or when someone ceased being unconditionally committed to their cause because they had been allegedly vanquished by individual values; she also reveals the movement's mechanisms of exclusion and rejection based on ethnicity and gender. What is particularly interesting is the dispute Aura Marina recalls having had with Régis Debray in Cuba when she tells him her critique of his book *Revolution within the Revolution*. Arriola considered the text to be a caricature of the events unfolding in the Latin American continent and describes how Debray not only failed to consider her as an equal (mirroring the attitude of other guerrilleros) but violently dismissed her comments on his theories. Similarly, Yolanda Colom explains that one of the problems of the movement was the reproduction of heteropatriarchy's toxic patterns. It becomes clear that both lived their condition as women as a handicap for their militant struggle, an obstacle for their political work, as having determined their intellectual work, as well as its status. When they devoted themselves to the "universal" cause of socialism, they lived on their own skins the fundamental incompatibility between this movement and feminism. It is said that Alaíde Foppa was also not taken very seriously by their militant peers for being a(n elderly) woman. She joined the struggle in 1980 when she was sixty-seven years old, inspired by her children who decided to take up arms beside guerrilleros in the Guatemala Mountains. Alaíde was assigned small intelligence tasks, but she was never prepared and never given instructions or protocol to protect herself when she was assigned a mission in Guatemala in 1980. Perhaps her age and her upper-class status of university professor exiled in Mexico were factors that influenced the fact that the movement put her at risk without intending to. Alaíde disappeared in December 1980 in Guatemala when her car was intercepted by agents from the Guatemalan army downtown in Guatemala City; two years later she was declared dead, her body vanished, probably in a mass grave lying next to her driver.[4] Just like her Guatemalan successors, Tina Modotti had thrown herself completely into armed struggle, abandoning photography to join sides with the Republican army during the Spanish Civil War in the 1930s. Modotti shared a tragic destiny similar to her Latin American successors: exile, illness, depression, burnout, loneliness.

Women guerrilleras from Mexico have also written or given oral testimony of their years in the movement. They are not a few: Guadalupe Gladys López Hernández, Paquita Calvo Zapata, Raquel Gutiérrez, Erika Samora, Ana Maria Vera Smith, Lourdes Uranga, Margarita Muñoz Conde, Maria Elena Dávalos Montero, Lourdes Quiñones, Lula Rodríguez, Edna Ovale, Aurora Castillo, Alicia de los Ríos Medina. They were members of organizations like the Liga 23 de Septiembre, ANCR, MAR, FUZ, La Brigada Roja, and so on, that declared war against the State.[5]

Like their Guatemalan counterparts, the accounts of these women describe (among other things), how gender was an unspoken obstacle in their struggle. According to Lourdes Uranga, for instance, one of the main principles of the guerrilla was to construct a "new" man that excluded the concept of femininity (not to say women in general). Values that ruled the guerilla, such as sacrifice, generosity, courage, intelligence, Marxism, or strength, were considered male attributes. Uranga was a member of the FUZ (Frente Urbano Zapatista, or Urban Zapatista Front, active between 1969 and 1973), and she remembers that fellows sought to model themselves after the figure of "El Che," but since there was no feminine counterpart, women had to masculinize themselves, working very hard to belong, and, as she puts it, "to bury our contradictions." In the context of political projects of guerrilla groups in the 1970s, there was no specific politics for women's ordeals. For the Left, the main enemies were imperialism, the State, and the bourgeoisie; heteropatriarchy was far from being on their political horizon. I must note that this outdated Leftist position is exactly the one held by Mexican president Andrés Manuel López Obrador, who has defunded refugee programs for women victims of gender violence, ignored demands of families of disappeared and murdered women across the country, reinforced traditional gender roles inherent to the traditional Mexican family, and made misogynist comments in a country where the term *femicide* has been exchange currency since the 1990s.

Uranga further recounts that when she filed for divorce, her children were taken away, causing her great suffering, and self-critically states that joining the guerrilla was in retrospect a means to escape from her "guardian" (husband). Later on, she gained a gender consciousness and began to militate for feminism.[6] Similarly, Gladys López declares that she had not been aware in the 1960s and 1970s of the fact that women of her generation were confronted with heteropatriarchal family and societal expectations, at a time when women did not have the slightest possibility to express yearnings for justice, freedom, and equality. As in the 1910 Revolution, women were perceived somewhat as "complementary" participants, as "Marías," companions or sex-providers, although many fought for equality in training and for similar conditions for militancy as men. Many of the women involved in Leftist movements, however, did not see themselves directly in combat, killing enemies. Gladys, for instance, was more of a support base for the movement, working as a courier between prisoners in Lecumberri and the world outside. Her goal was to become a bridge of sorts, between the rural and urban guerrillas. She was in close contact, among others, with leaders of the Chicano movement and Black Panthers in the US (she got mail from Angela Davis while serving a sentence in Santa Marta Acatitla between 1971 and 1974). Like Gladys, other women participated by doing political and logistical analysis, finding supplies, or working as couriers. Lourdes Uranga notes the difference in social perception between men coming out of jail as heroes while female ex-prisoners were seen as vulgar and prosaic prostitutes and were thus rejected by society.

Escaping the role imposed on young women by heteropatriarchy was not the only (unconscious) reason for joining the guerrilla. Gladys López tells in her memoir titled *Ovarynomy* (as opposed to *testi(cle)mony*) that she was secretly enrolled in the Preparatoria Popular because her parents did not allow her to pursue high school studies. The Preparatoria Popular was founded in 1968 in Mexico City by students from the Philosophy and Literature Department at the National Autonomous University (UNAM) to accept students rejected from public or UNAM high schools or who otherwise were unable to enroll. The UNAM recognized the school officially and gave them a battered building in the Juárez neighborhood in Mexico City. Lourdes Uranga also studied in secret; she had married at nineteen and began to pursue an undergraduate degree in social work. After the events of October 1968, of which she had been a survivor and witness in Tlatelolco, she decided to join the urban guerrilla. As a matter of fact, many young people began to radicalize against the government's "hard hand" after they experienced State violence on their own skins after the October 1968 massacre, and thus began the Dirty War. Uranga made a decision to join the FUZ, created in 1969, and was trained in urban guerrilla fighting, which included learning judo, karate, weapon use, and driving. On September 21, 1971, she took part in the kidnapping of Julio Hirschfeld Almada, director of the government institution Aeropuertos and Servicios Auxiliares (Airports and Auxiliary Services), for a three-million-peso ransom for the cause. Like Gladys López (and others), Lourdes Uranga was detained, tortured, and imprisoned in Santa Marta Acatitla.[7] As part of a prisoner exchange, Uranga was exiled to Cuba, then to Italy. In 1979 the Mexican government gave amnesty to political prisoners and she came back to become a professor at the Chapingo University, also becoming active in the feminist movement.

Guerrilleros and guerrilleras began to be detained in 1972, and a year later forced disappearances began, which was the case for the majority of militants like Alicia de los Ríos Merino and Amanda Arciniega Cano, members of the Liga 23 de Septiembre who were "disappeared" by the DFS (Dirección Federal de Seguridad or Federal Security Agency) around 1978. For the duration of the Dirty War, the press did not ascribe any social, political, or ideological grounds to armed groups; confrontations, kidnappings, and forced disappearances were reported in the "nota roja," newspaper sections for police reports informing about political movements' actions as crimes.

Although these women do not comply with the canonical standards of celebrity, it is necessary to honor their struggle and work, to learn from them. Guerrilleras have had to live with the psychological consequences of the brutal repression, to process the sequelae of torture, jail, and repression, of having placed the collective above individual interests of their own. Their social rebelliousness in challenging the State must be acknowledged as a costly effort to change the world.

Comparing these women's stories to "being a vegetarian lesbian" as a site of political enunciation (as is senator and cabaret performer Jesusa Rodrí- guez's position), or the transfiguration of militancy into cultural activism— or worse: into social media activism—implies the liquidation of Leftist mili- tancy and historical revisionism. We need to recuperate their stories, their voices, and turn up their sound, so that we can drown out prevailing prob- lematic revisionist voices that discredit the political work by Leftist militants half a century ago, for instance, the problematic voice of Colombian former presidential candidate for the Partido Verde Oxígeno (Oxygen Green Party) Ingrid Betancourt. In the 1990s, Betancourt began to denounce corruption in Colombia and became active, seeking to end the links between drug traf- ficking and politicians. During her 2002 presidential campaign, Betancourt travelled to Guaviare, a tropical rainforest region in Colombia considered to be of high risk by her bodyguards and the government at the time. She was taken prisoner and held captive for six years, after which the government rescued her along with fourteen other prisoners in a major military opera- tion. Her book *No hay silencio que no termine* (2010; *Even Silence Has an End: My Six Years of Captivity*) is her memoir of the strict regime to which she was subjected to during her captivity.[8] Describing emotions ranging from dignity to anger, Betancourt tells in detail the tortures she was sub- ject to, the small luxuries she found to make her ordeal less difficult, like listening to the radio show through which her family sent her messages, her escape attempts, and the French lessons she imparted to other prisoners. She describes situations such as being tied to a tree by the neck with a chain outdoors in the tropical jungle, her mental and physical ailments, the thou- sands of ways her captors humiliated her and tried to take her dignity away, the means of psychological manipulation that promoted tensions amongst the prisoners, the aftereffects of the kidnapping. Betancourt sums up her experience as the first time in her whole life that she had felt fear and that she had been defeated by terror, and that is what makes her keep on going.[9] From fear and hatred (which are emotions that none of the guerrilleras, in the accounts I have read and heard, have allowed themselves), Betancourt seeks to regain and preserve her individual integrity above all, denouncing the corruption of the ideals of Leftists' collective armed struggle. We should not be surprised that her book has been compared to Aleksandr Solzhenit- syn's *Gulag Archipelago* (1974), a narrative that brought to a crisis the inter- national Stalinist Left by denouncing repression and other Soviet régime vices supposedly unknown in the rest of the world. Betancourt tirelessly reveals the ideological distortion, the evil, the reality of corruption and loss of ideals behind the FARC struggles. But beyond her denunciations and defeat by fear, to me her voice represents a rupture with the possibility of imagining a better world from the standpoint of the Left. To me, it signifies the rendition of the Left before the horror of the reality of capitalism, but worst of all, it represents the privatization of collective struggles as a spurious solution to survive within the current reality. In Betancourt, as fear defeats love and the individual wins over collective struggle, her obsession with individual security and well-being are put above the common good. When comparing Betancourt's writings with Colom, Arriola, López, or Uranga, it is interesting noting how the women from the previous generation describe their sacrifices for militancy in a radically different way than Betancourt. Without a doubt, Betancourt succumbs to extreme states of anxiety, showing her absolute subjection to neoliberal structures of domination. Clearly fear promotes the desire for privatizing everything as well as the belief that safety can always be found in sameness. The alterity that seems to threaten Betancourt is the apparent ideological distortion of Leftist struggle manifested in the perversity of the post-ideological paramilitary movement of Latin American guerrillas. The same de-ideologization and alleged lack of meaning of guerrilla struggles is also registered in *Monos*, the film by Alejandro Landes (Ecuador/Colombia 2019). The movie is a fable of a group of guerrillero children immersed in a world of war and adolescence supervised by a feared "Messenger" who gives them orders on behalf of the "Organization." The Messenger orders them to look out for "la Doctora," a US citizen who has been kidnapped for ransom. The kids fool around sexually, do capoeira, experiment with hallucinogens, play with their weapons, fight for leadership, and establish a hierarchy among themselves. While the film has no geographical, political, or historical reference points, the situation speaks of contemporary Colombia, where guerrillas are discredited and criminalized. In the film, the group of guerrillero teenagers in the jungle play at war for war's sake (as is the neoliberal discourse of territorial defense struggles), and thus the teenagers' community appears as a dystopian or aberrant form of human existence, devoid of values and purpose, incapable of surviving beyond social Darwinism, akin to William Golding's 1954 novel *Lord of the Flies*.

But aren't all combatants legal or illegal sadists who use torture methods and other forms of subjection against the enemy, the State for instance? The "Doctora" in *Monos* goes through an ordeal similar to Betancourt's. Like her, she fails to escape twice, she is physically and psychologically tortured and there is an episode with a pair of rubber boots that recalls one narrated by Betancourt in her memoir. The erasure of originary peoples in struggles due to racism and five centuries of colonialism is hidden—partly due to the inadequacy of Leftist ideology to change the world—and this is how armed guerrillas appear as evil in both the film and in Betancourt's memoir. What is also erased from both narratives is how the white women are perceived by their captors: as foreigners, invaders, and enemies. What we are allowed to see are their good Leftist intentions and then the disappointment and abandonment of such intentions in the process of their captivity due to the distortion of the struggle of "others" with whom they can no longer empathize.

Laurence Debray's voice is akin to Betancourt's as she affirms the values of individualism while reviling Leftist militancy of the twentieth century. In her book, *Hija de revolucionarios* (2018; *Daughter of revolutionaries*), she narrates how her parent's militancy (Elizabeth Burgos and Régis Debray) determined her childhood and her decisions as adult. The text is reminiscent of Julie Gavras' film *La faute à Fidel* (2006; *Blame it on Fidel*). Julie Gavras is revolutionary filmmaker Costa Gavras' daughter, and her film tells the story of a nine-year-old whose parents turn themselves to the Leftist militant struggle supporting France Allende's government in Chile. Her mother, a reporter for *Marie Claire*, becomes a feminist militant and begins writing a book gathering testimonies of abortion. From one day to the next, the child is forced to renounce the life of privileges that she has until then known, to move to a working-class apartment mostly full of *barbus* (men with beards, an adjective given to Leftist militants at the time), feminists, and refugees, and where bohemian nights, refugee nannies, and international food become the norm along with completely new household rules that startle her constantly. Like the character in Gavras' film, Laurence Debray is forced as a child to live the contradictions inherent to her parent's Leftist militant lifestyles. Curiously for both, their grandparents represent the lost bourgeois paradise the girls come to as a refuge.

In her book, Laurence tells episodes of her own life interlinked with that of the myth of her revolutionary parents. Both adhered to the Tricontinental program in 1965, which attempted to foment a world revolution to destabilize US imperialism and emancipate the oppressed of the whole world. The couple moved to Cuba that year, where Debray wrote the aforementioned book *Revolución en la revolución* (criticized by Arriola) while Burgos was trained as a spy. In 1967, Régis Debray joined Che Guevara's guerrilla movement in Bolivia, was detained, and served a four-year-long prison sentence; once he was liberated, he came back to France to devote himself to writing. When François Mitterrand came to power, Debray was named president's advisor, and Elizabeth Burgos became director of the Maison de l'Amérique Latine. Burgos, Laurence Debray's mother, is a Venezuelan militant who has devoted her life to the ideals of the Left. She met Debray in 1967 and led the campaign for his liberation from jail in Bolivia. She is also known for having co-written Rigoberta Menchú's biography, the Guatemalan woman of Mayan origin who won a Nobel Peace Prize in 1992. From the beginning, Laurence expresses resentment against her father for having made her grandparents suffer when the calumny of his death alongside Che Guevara became public. She also expresses anger for what it meant for her as a child to live with parents engaged with the June 21, 1981, Association. This institution sought through diplomacy to defend human rights in third world countries, attempting, for instance, to free the political prisoners of dictatorial regimes (in Brazil, Argentina, Chile, Uruguay, Bolivia, Iran) from jails, get them visas, and organize mass media campaigns. Laurence laments that her parent's endless political work and their engagement with Leftist ideals prevented them from living carefree with illusions; she accuses them of rejecting fashion and comfort, of living their power as a duty and not as a privilege, of allowing her to consume only what is useful and basic, of resisting the times, national celebrations, easy things—and of "carrying the weight of the world over their shoulders, especially the Third World."[10] Laurence's stand can be summed up in the way in which she declares her differentiation from her parents: "my parents embraced great political ideals to try to guide the good sense of the curse of history; I have preferred to look after my health and my children's well-being."[11] Predictably, she ends up writing a book about the Spanish monarchy and working at the New York stock exchange (a job that she had to quit after September 11, 2001, when procedures to get a visa to live or work in the US were hardened: Debray was denied her visa because of her parents' status as prominent Leftists). Like Betancourt, Laurence Debray turns to the private realm, embracing the neoliberal values of the privatization of political problems and thus individual struggle, the self's well-being, the cultivation of the I.

Of course I'm not interested in doing an idealist defense of revolutionary struggles from the second half of the twentieth century; their failures are well known—for instance, their blindness toward heteropatriarchy and their current obsolescence under renewed extractivist neofeudalist forces, but above all, their helplessness in the face of sophisticated repression techniques across the world. To think only about reverting to armed struggle or violence to take overpower is ridiculous in part because "power" no longer resides in the State but in invisible institutions, in insidious and malignant structures of subjectivation that spread through semiotic fluxes in the infosphere, through personal and national debt, digital infrastructure, the ubiquity of the relationality crisis. And without going deeper into the dangers of what it would imply to get weapons or intelligence to effectively attack the State, we can take Julian Assange or other whistleblowers as examples: the consequences Chelsea Manning, Anat Karam, and Edward Snowden faced as exemplars, punished to deter the rest of the world from approaching the underbelly of power.

What interests me in comparing guerrillera testimonies to Betancourt's and Debray's is that the contrast reveals the fact of the turn of political struggles to the private sphere which goes hand in hand with the dissociation between theory and practice and with the transformation of militancy into cultural intervention: what we could consider the problematic zero degree of the "bureaucratization of the vanguards." Another issue that rises when I read guerrillera testimonies alongside Betancourt and Debray is, What is the meaning of Leftist values in this society? How have these values (equality, liberation from State oppression, anticapitalism, self-sacrifice for the common good) mutated? What is the place of the "Third World" and Indigenous peoples in Leftist struggles beyond being considered by ecological movements as the guardians of the planet or being recognized as self-determined cultural (not political) subjects? Clearly the enterprise of the Left from the second half of the twentieth century was the failed project of a generation moved by a dream or illusion inherited from the Enlightenment that sought to palliate the effects of colonization with the principles of a libertarian humanism supported by the intellectual class. But beyond that, the link between thought and political action has been clearly broken: the figures who have public influence today are no longer political or intellectual referents but sports players, celebrities, influencers, and commentators who move the masses with passion, just like the State, which functions like a spectacle to hide and thus legitimate the mortal effects of the neoliberal economy. This means that the State operates through symbols and by establishing a language and distance between stage and public, immersing itself directly in the masses, live. In this context, the expectations that we have of the leading class are alienation and partisanship, the administration of collective emotions and public services as well as the imposition of a clientelist neopopulist relationship to the State. As a remnant of Enlightenment values, we still believe that with critical thought, reason, and the demonstration of written arguments, we can interpret and thus transform the world, and that unfair societies can be rendered equal through legislation, economic measures, and policy. But we forget that inequality was created by centuries-old structures of domination grounded on a predatory culture. Although we live in close contact with neighbors among the masses of people from our society, we feel alienated, lonely. Isolation and solitude are the main causes of depression and desperation and are the result of lives lived in a society in which the "I" matters more than the rest. The *buen vivir* is no longer rooted in community and in connection with others, but in accumulation and fulfillment of hedonist and materialist desires.

This is why the rich and famous are seen as the relevant cultural icons or referents in our societies over intellectuals, leaders, and political activists. Veneration for money expresses itself in the reality of turning a blind eye to corruption; we accept the lack of ethics in politicians' and bureaucrats' support for corporations and monopolies, imperialism, and crony capitalism based on enrichment by family or friendship ties, the substitution of the "mafia in power" in spite of the declared purity of Andrés Manuel López Obrador's government. We are beyond nostalgia for the loss of unity, for the disappearance of tradition, for yearning after true moral guides. We have failed to inherit the history of Leftist struggles and their repression, because we have forgotten them (buried indeed by power), but above all, because now it is too easy to satisfy our good intentions without needing to consider joining any kind of movement, let alone the guerrilla. What are reflection, reason, thought for if they are not helping to bring back the disappeared; aid the refugees, the displaced, those fighting for their territories; to condemn torturers, prosecutors, and oppressors?

Another of the issues that comes up when thinking about revolutionary struggles of the past is the current disconnection and lack of solidarity between politicized urban movements and their rural counterparts. Among other reasons, this is due to prejudice, racism, the "bad reputation" that rural movements have gained either for being inspired by obsolete ideologies or for threatening the rule of law—even if in self-defense. For instance, two comparable cases (and exemplary models of neoliberal toxic masculinity) that show this disconnection and prejudice are José Manuel Mireles, leader of the Grupos de Autodefensa Comunitaria (Community Self-Defense Groups) who fought against the Caballeros Templarios cartel in the state of Michoacán, and Mauricio Fernández, mayor of the San Pedro Garza García municipality in Monterrey, Nuevo León (the richest gated community in Latin America) for three terms, the last between 2009 and 2012. Both leaders turned to extralegal measures to defend their communities from organized crime, but while Mireles went to jail (his destiny was privileged in comparison to that of other community police leaders or territorial defense leaders), Mauricio Fernández's paramilitary measures were profusely celebrated by the elite he protected.[12] The disconnect between struggles for the defense of territory in rural areas and urban struggles for rights, antagonism, visibility, security, and restitution make it so that Indigenous movements and their leaders are considered to be representing a different politics, on the side or that in some way doesn't count. That is why it is important to acknowledge other forms of resistance, for instance, the ways Indigenous leaders like Martha Sánchez Néstor and the Comandante Nestora Salgado (an ex-commander of communal police of the CRAC-PC in Olinalá) have not only fought for their rights and defense of their territories but are also an example of women struggling to undo the gender habitus in their communities.[13]

As a basis for the very necessary experiment of interweaving originary peoples' struggles for territorial defense with matters that concern urban populations (like housing, water, rights, jobs, etc., —and soon there will be struggles for fuel and food), there is the "feminist strike," theorized by Verónica Gago. Parting from recent experiences in Argentina and the rest of Latin America, the political tool of the strike is deterritorialized from the working class to be appropriated by feminists to confront the financialization of life, the production of debt, and the new forms of exploitation of social and natural extractivism. According to Gago, the feminist strike is a process rather than a movement that maps out new forms of exploitations of bodies and territories visibilizing the machinery of precarity upon which the system is sustained. With the strike, the feminist struggle goes beyond the realm of domestic violence to connect with economic, labor, institutional, police, racist, and colonial violences, interweaving the relationships among these violences with financial and territorial extractivism.[14] The feminist strike draws a map of conflicts that go beyond the frontiers between life and work, body and territory, law and violence. The tool of the strike, traditionally associated with workers' union struggles, as a site of action places women, lesbians, bisexuals, and trans and nonbinary people as political subjects beyond the position of victims seeking rights or restitution from the State by drawing a connection between gender violences, reproductive labor, and financial exploitation. The exercise of subtraction and mass sabotage occurred for the first time in Argentina in March 2016, then 2017 and 2018, and in 2019 the strike began to expand throughout Latin America, concatenating November 25 or the Día internacional de la Eliminación de la Violencia Contra las Mujeres (International Day for the Elimination of Violence against Women) (the date was established during the First Latin American and Caribbean Feminist Encounter celebrated in

Bogotá in 1981 and made official by the UN). Both events were interlinked through the hashtags #NiUnaMás (Not one more), #VivasNosQueremos (We want ourselves alive), #ElVioladorEresTú (You are the rapist), the legalization of abortion, and so on. Insubordination from the feminist perspective overflows the workspace because it not only paralyzes productive work, but it also halts normal life, sexual division of labor, the political arbitrariness that organizes the borders between work and nonwork, and the structures and mandates that make capitalism possible.[15]

From *Las niñas bien* to the *Primates of Park Avenue*

In a text from 1985, Félix Guattari and Toni Negri discuss "the becoming middle class of the communist idea," which in their view, had been appropriated as a slogan by politicians, academics, artists.[1] The becoming middle class of the communist idea implies the rise of a cultivated and politicized middle class with a Leftist sensibility (the liberal class) but lacking real connection with the poor, the working class, originary peoples, migrants, and exploited people. Communism had become a metaphor that didn't exist as an actual thing anymore, giving way to a "cultural Left" that would begin to adhere to the ethical principles of human rights and the rights of visibility and recognition of minorities. The becoming middle class of the communist idea transformed Leftist politics and became exchange currency to achieve privileges and visibility, putting on the side not only the idealism of class struggle, but also the connection with "the people" and organized militancy. Two years after Guattari and Negri's diagnosis, *Las niñas bien* was published in Mexico, a text by Guadalupe Loaeza without characters or a plot that narrates in a journalistic style and with autobiographical hues the life of privileged women (*niñas bien*) in Mexico in the first person and at the verge of a series of economic crises that would shake the country in the following decade. It doesn't go without saying that the hermetic Mexican bourgeoisies could only be narrated from the inside at the moment in which it was about to collapse. Loeaza's book is an inventory of customs as habits, social rituals, of the minutia of a certain class consciousness, their values, but also of the restrictions under which rich women had lived without university education or being able to drive their own car, have bank accounts in their names, or make transcendental decisions in their lives let alone join street protests, vote, work, and make money. Relegated to being guardians of family values and perpetuating social relations to reproduce their own class privileges so their children could inherit them, the mission of *las niñas bien* was to protect and transmit, generation after generation, the customs they had inherited along with their collections of luxury objects and other paraphernalia legitimating their class status. Customs and habits, which are the sum of repertoires and protocols, gestures and lifestyles, had been copied from the court of Louis XIV as a form of life to justify the upper class's social place above the rest of society: the know-how of being served and of recognizing and relating to people who are similar to themselves.

Loeaza's texts were adapted to film by director Alejandra Márquez. The result is *Las niñas bien* (2019) a fiction about the crumbling of the Mexican industrial bourgeoisie caused by the liberalization of the market under the government of José López Portillo. The establishment of neoliberal politics in Mexico implied the advent of a new oligarchy (what is known as the 1 percent) who would make a fortune with privatization, State concessions, real estate, financial economy, mass media, transnational corporations, technology, digital platforms and apps, and the neofeudalist extractivist economy. It must be noted that this oligarchy or plutocracy is global; it exists in communist China and Russia as it does in functional social democracies like Sweden, Finland, or Germany, and even in Third World banana republics like Congo, Mexico, or Brazil.

In Márquez's film, Sofía is a *niña bien* who observes how the family enterprise directed by her husband goes bankrupt because he is too childish to step up and face the new economic challenges brought by the liberalization of the market. In the film, we see Sofía losing her privileges gradually—her credit card doesn't go through, she doesn't have enough money to hire ponies for her children's birthday party, she has to buy clothes in a local department store as opposed to doing her trimestral shopping pilgrimage to New York, she runs out of cash to pay her domestic workers. . . . All the while, we see Sofía's mix of disdain and anxiety before the ways Ana Paula, a member of the nouveau riche, is trying to win her friendship and that of her cadre to be able to belong to the high society circle of *las niñas bien*. Márquez's film registers the disappearance of the twentieth-century Mexican industrial bourgeoisie and the fall of families who had been rich and in power *de toda la vida* (privileged people whose ancestors knew each other), replaced by the incipient global plutocracy of capitalist cronies. A similar reconversion is recorded in Guadalupe Amor's *Yo soy mi casa* (1956; I am my home).[2] Amor's only book written in prose is neither a memoir or a novel; she reminisces about her childhood, marked by the family's loss of their hacienda in Morelos to Zapatista hands during the Mexican Revolution and the book is thus a portrait of aristocratic decadence spiraling downward on the scale of high society.

While the voice in *Yo soy mi casa* describes how her family tries to keep up appearances through various means from a young girl's point of view, in Loaeza, the repertoire of protocols, gestures, and habits carefully transmitted from generation to generation by women (along with Christofle cutlery, fine Baccarat crystal, Venetian glass, jewelry, and heirlooms) stop making sense, opening up to a new series of codes of belonging to the privileged social spheres.

Unlike the bourgeois industrialized class who owned the means of production and conceded rights to workers thanks to pressure exercised by workers' movements and government intervention, the new class of the super-rich emerged through tax exceptions, privatization, and the lack of protection and guarantees for workers. To the reasons for the emergence of the new oligarchy we can add the technological revolution and globalization as opportunities for enrichment and what is known as crony capitalism. The idea that with intelligence and luck anyone can quickly become a billionaire is widely spread and is exemplified by people like David Kar, founder of Tumblr, who sold his company to Yahoo for $1.1 billion when he was twenty-six years old.

In her book *Plutocrats: The Rise of the New Global Super-Rich* (2012) journalist Chyrstia Freeland notes that income inequality is nowadays particularly deep between those on top and everyone else. In fact, the income gap between the 1 percent and the 10 percent top earners is exponentially wider than the difference between the income of the 10 percent and the rest of the population. Considering that the 1 percent earns 80 percent of income at the global level, this situation has no precedents in history. The 1 percent includes celebrities who can be actors, athletes, musicians who have been enabled to expand their talents across the globe thanks to new technologies, creating a sub-caste of "super-star service providers" made up of technicians, lawyers, architects, chefs, dentists. We should consider, however, that what thirty years ago was a meritocratic plutocracy has now become a crony plutocracy: now if you are not born as one of the 1 percent it has become very difficult to join the race to ascend. We could talk about a kind of social Darwinism in which those above have established themselves as the new dominant oligarchy having left the weakest behind (or below). The 1 percent are like the characters in the movie and book *Crazy Rich*

Asians, the HBO series *Succession*, or Wednesday Martin's anthropological chronicle *Primates of Park Avenue* (2015), and they all represent the neoliberal reconversion of *las niñas bien*. In her book, Martin gave herself the task of revealing the secrets of New York's Upper East Side wives and mothers.[3] Her book documents the formulas of social climbing in relationship to fashion, formality, and conservatism exhibited by these primates, the protocols to being accepted, and the social codes operating in the elites' private schools. There is a whole chapter devoted to how to buy property in the Upper East Side, including the process of getting approval for the buying family by the building's neighbors council; another chapter tells the mishaps the author goes through to be able to buy a Birkin bag. Apparently Hermés choses its clients, not shoppers the product, as the bag represents a mark of exclusivity and belonging. To be able to buy one, a recommendation and a complicated request protocol are necessary. In a way, the plutocrat's rituals are no longer tied to ancestry or lineage but to their consumption elections and spending capacity, the spaces they inhabit and the events where they socialize. The mothers at the preschool the anthropologist's son attends to all wear Lululemon sports clothing and Prada high heels as well as carrying Birkin bags. Martin reports that women from this class either work or are provided for and obtain "bonuses" from their husbands according to their performance as mothers (reflected through their children's success) and as wives (for instance, if they manage to keep themselves in shape). These women administer homes as efficiently as big corporations (for which they probably stopped working at some point in their married lives).

Nothing could be further away from the world of French nuns, New York shopping trips, domestic workers impeccably dressed in matching uniforms, béchamel sauces, and starched tablecloths from forty years ago. Another important difference is that the old industrial bourgeoisie came with its own antidote to social inequality: communism, an alternative to capitalist society positing forth a utopian horizon and a frame for the struggle for equality. In fact, many of the most prominent communists from the twentieth century came from bourgeois families.

In a 2019 exhibition in Mexico City at the Kurimanzutto Gallery in Mexico City, *El placer después (Pleasure Afterwards)*, artist Miguel Calderón showed a series of watercolors, an installation of old gas tanks wearing jewelry made of dog food, drawings, and a film that tells a story dealing with our current society's incapacity to deal with class difference and social tensions. The video tells the story of a warden who works for the Cibeles roundabout in the Roma neighborhood in Mexico City who got trapped inside the machine room after the September 19, 2017, earthquake. Before that, he had wanted to take revenge against the owners of the neighborhood's dogs because they never clean up after them, that is why he tried to feed the dogs poisoned food that he carried in his pockets. After the earthquake though, he was found by a rescue dog thanks to the smell of the food he had on himself. The workers then decided to always have dog food on them in case there is another earthquake. The dogs have been forgiven, but not their owners. That is why in Calderón's video, three of the Cibeles fountain workers invade the apartment of one of the filthy owners and secretly perform all kinds of denigrating actions and gestures expressing their hatred toward the "señora," like licking all of her furniture.

The video (unintentionally) makes evident a lack of discourse or frame in the socio-political horizon to channel tensions generated by class difference and for imagining possibilities to close the gaps between them; the discourses of the violation of human rights (which divides society into victims and aggressors) and populist hatred against everything perceived as *fifí* (snobbish; everything pertaining to the middle class or the petit bourgeoisie) falls evidently short, and this situation represents two centuries' regression in terms of political work. While Miguel Calderon's exhibition was up, at few blocks distant, at Labor, British artist Yuri Patterson's installation *Crisis Cast (Public Solitude)* was displayed. In its own way, Patterson's installation also deals with social tensions that have no visible resolution but that are handled through technological solutions. The installation comprises a surveillance apparatus that records images in real time in the gallery that visitors see projected on a screen. The feed is edited haphazardly into a second video that shows a group of "crisis administrators" who work for a British security company. The "crisis administrators" were hired by Patterson to do a mise en scène of their work for a performance. They are actors who have been trained by the company Crisis Cast to be ready to take action in any situation of man-made or natural disaster. They are part of the technical infrastructure for handling terrorist attacks or natural disasters. Pattison asked the Crisis Cast to simulate a surveillance situation at an airport inside a half-built theater in London. The video is shot from different perspectives and at some moments it simulates the neutral gaze of CCTV cameras. If in Miguel Calderon's *El placer después*, social differences are source of polarization, disrespect, hatred, and vengeance, in Yuri Pattison's installation, paranoia of imminent threat and loneliness are posited as mediators of social relations and class and racial tensions in public spaces.

Four decades ago, political action had as a goal to bring down bourgeois power and instaurate socialism. People of Leftist sensibility sought coherence in their political stand and everyday lives, sometimes bearing weapons on their hands. For one of the essays in her collection *Fuerte es el silencio* (1980; Strong is the silence), Elena Poniatowska interviews Paquita Calvo Zapata, the guerrillera for the Frente Urbano Zapatista (FUZ or Zapatista Urban Front), at the woman's prison Santa Marta Acatitla.[4] Based in Mexico City, the FUZ attacked twice: they assaulted the Banco de México (Del Valle branch) in 1970, and a year later, as I discussed, they kidnapped Julio Hirschfield Almada. Paquita tells Elenita that the failure of the FUZ was due to their disconnection from the masses, their inability to bridge peasants' and the working class's struggles. A second encounter, with a liberated Paquita, is the pretext for an extraordinary passage written by Elena, in which she posits the era's conundrum: the incipient collectivization of consumption and narcissism contrasting with the harsh social reality represented by Paquita's struggle:

> Because Paquita, who has been released, lives nearby the Palacio de Hierro, I thought: "It's great because when I leave her home, I can pass by the store and see what I can find, a little shirt, an undergarment, underwear, perhaps a skirt." [. . .] Now I myself am part of that multitude galloping toward Palacio de Hierro, I belong to this homogenous society and I am easily recognizable as a person who paws and acts without good sense on wooden floors, pushing others between the counters, hissing, rummaging, looking for what? I am the general public who responds to the sales announcement, General Sale, Sales valid from July 22–26, over 30 percent discount on these dresses sizes 12 to 22, models very appropriate for the summer season, in materials that are easy to clean, 100% polyester, they come in short sleeves, sports neck, and original patterns in fashionable colors.[5]

Elenita asks herself if this incipient consumer society opposes the guerrilla, and what would happen if a guerrillero would enter a misery–belt shack, "Would he shut the family's TV off and lecture the eight people sitting on a single bed on socialism, would they listen to him? Would they consider change as an asset? Freedom as an asset? What are for them life's assets? Are they not those that can be bought?"[6]

The spirit of the times is absolutely foreign today, yet we have inherited the unresolved contradictions of class struggle and now live under the neoliberal regime of social Darwinism in which plutocrats demarcate themselves from the rest by isolating themselves in gated communities, consuming luxury experiences and objects in a world that begins to manifest itself as total environmental ruin denied by a visionless ruling class. As in New York's Park Avenue, the law of the strongest predominates in the Amazon

FIGURE 2. Elsa-Louise Manceaux, *Idéal Number Five* (2016), photo by Fabiola Menchelli, courtesy of the artist.

rainforest jungle. The fires in 2019 that destroyed an important portion of the jungle were in truth an act of civil disobedience by landowners who wanted to appropriate portions of land owned by the Jamanxím Jungle National Reserve in at the Pará province in Brazil. They organized to deforest it with the fires to build infrastructure for cattle pastures to export meat. The ranchers are seeking to privatize the reserve and to open up the Amazon for "development," seeking to "satisfy our needs, not the world's needs."

In the meantime, in Ecuador, thousands of Indigenous peoples marched to the capital to protest the adscription of the government presided over by Lénin Moreno to a reform package prescribed to Ecuador by the International Monetary Fund. Quito was militarized, there was chaos throughout the country, and it was reported that Lenin Moreno abandoned the capital to establish a temporary siege of his government in Guayaquil. Before this landscape, Indigenous autonomies and the feminist strike theorized by Verónica Gago can be seen as very much needed and urgent tools to explore forms of politicization in synch with the problems we are facing today beyond useless institutional mechanisms provided by Leftist ideology and the State for that effect.

Mangomitas Postcard

A few weeks ago, in the bulk candy aisle at the supermarket, I was struggl-ing to fill a cellophane bag with mangomitas (a kind of soft mango-flavored candy covered in powdered chili) with a pair of plastic tongs (mental note: next time bring a plastic container to not create waste by using the cello-phane bag). The catch was that my left arm was in a sling, which made the task enormously difficult. I had been able to place, slowly and one by one, three mangomitas in the bag, but in the following attempt I put too much pressure on the tongs, spilling a bunch of sweets onto the floor. Ashamed and uncomfortable, I resisted the impulse to pick them up with my right hand, and I used the tongs to place them carefully on the bag. I was absorbed by this enormously difficult task, when an elder woman, older than my mother, around seventy years old, came toward me to offer me her help. "If we don't help each other, then who will? And especially today," she told me with a smile. I felt like crying of relief, of sadness. We need to resist our feeling of alienation, exhaustion, to see each other more, to get together to conspire, to denaturalize indifference beyond March 8. A few weeks later, I was crossing the street, arm liberated and in rehabilitation, leading my stepdogs on a busy street at La Roma. They trotted happily before me as usual, and when we were about to cross, the cars had a green light but the density of the traffic made it impossible for them to move forward; there was a gap between cars, so I took up the chance to go forward but a man in a car advanced toward me. When I saw half of Rocco end up beneath the front of his car, I felt assaulted and was furious, so I turned around and yelled (self-aware of needing to control my anger, LOL), "Be more careful!" When I got to the other end, I saw a woman in her early thirties (now I'm wondering if I'm good at calculating other people's ages since I seem to do it so comfortably here); she walked toward the cab still stuck in traffic and began kicking it and yelling at the driver, "Son of a bitch! Watch where you are going! You almost ran over her dog!" She was defending me. She was angrier than me, for me. And I thought, we are all *encabronadas* (pissed off) together. A few weeks later, the famous women's march protesting gender violence would end up with accusations of vandalism. Feminists were dismissed for being hooligans because some of the protesters drew graffiti over national monuments, most notably the Ángel de la Independencia in the emblematic Reforma Avenue in Mexico City. The symbolic action went over the fiscals' and critics' heads: monuments serve to dress and legitimize the fatherland, which is in principle, misogynist. That is why in Las Tesis' chant "El violador eres tú" the finger is pointing at the heteropatriarchal State. After George Floyd's murder, protests also came with vandalism or tearing down of monuments and statues throughout the US. Indeed monuments and statues represent state power and this is why our relationship to them is emotional and unconscious, because for better or worse, they are part of our history. In the national narratives embodied by history, monuments, and public spaces, women and minorities are almost never included. National heroes are mostly white males and monuments embody this point of view of national history. Vandalizing and tearing them down is a means to demand a revision of the history that backs up oppressive power structures and narratives.

One on One: LakeVerea vs. Bellas Artes

A photography exhibition by the collective LakeVerea, formed by Francisca Rivero Lake and Carla Verea, took place from September to November 2019 at the Bellas Artes Palace in Mexico City. Their point of departure was establishing a dialogue with the architecture of the Palace based on the premise of the inaccessibility of the Palace's monumental (but also conceptual and historical) elements for the majority of its visitors. For that purpose, the artists did research about the building, conceived in an era in which Italy and France were key referents of high culture and vanguard, and when the identity of modern Mexico was conceived as essentially *mestizo*, that is to say, embodying its pre-Hispanic past and Europeanized present. Central to LakeVerea's dialogue with the Palace is to "bring close to the viewer what is out of her reach by reconfiguring the Palace's spatial discourse." The artists thus proposed physical and direct confrontations with photographed select details of the Palace: immense figureheads, doors, adornments, sculptures, and murals. Then, they played with the size and the visual outreach of the reproductions using photography as a tool to make accessible "moments" or "fragments" of the Palace to the viewers. For instance, the Tláloc figurehead, the metal doors, the marble sculptures; a detail from a female character in José Clemente Orozco's mural or the eclipse from Tamayo's mural. The discourse of the exhibition is accessibility through a didactic and inclusive approach to the Bellas Artes Palace's architecture and decorative elements: the text at the entrance wall is read in sign language in a video in an adjacent screen; the blind may touch the art deco alphabet of the Palace's typography reproduced in another of the walls.

FIGURE 3. Photograph of the exhibition *LakeVerea vs. Bellas Artes* (2019), © LakeVerea.

A "shero" offered guided tours for children, and on another wall, there was a graphic explaining the visual and spatial logic of perspective to visitors.

For LakeVerea, the monumentality of the Palace disguises its elitism and machismo, and that is why the discourse of accessibility in the exhibition functions as a Trojan horse of sorts to make a queer critical reading of official patrimony and art from Mexican history: "size does matter," and the Palace's dimension is one of the discourses through which State power legitimizes itself. Not by chance, the Bellas Artes Palace was one of the monuments chosen to be heavily armored for the day of the feminist march against gender violence on November 25, 2019. If these kinds of buildings represent the patrimony of a nation, indeed they materialize and guarantee the perpetuation of heteropatriarchy. In one of the photographs, LakeVerea show themselves behind a photographic camera measuring themselves "one to one" against one of the Palace's columns, trying to understand its dimension, color, smell, and temperature but also announcing their queer and feminist gaze.[1] In the photograph that reproduces a fragment of Rufino Tamayo's mural *Nacimiento de nuestra nacionalidad* (1952), we see an eclipse that can be interpreted as the poetic fusion during the encounter between two bodies, be them celestial, human, or cultural. From David Alfaro Siqueiros' mural *La tortura de Cuauhtémoc* (1951–52), they framed Malinche's tongue. In the mural, Malinche appears speaking to the ear of one of the conquistadores, and in LakeVerea's photograph, the tongue is isolated as an erotic element alluding to the role Malinche played in the Spanish conquest of Mexico, but also to her strength, intelligence, and multilingual skills. From Siqueiros' mural *Katharsis* (1934–35), LakeVerea framed the face of a woman who appears lying down on the floor naked with her legs spread open. Her face bears a sinister laugher enclosed by pearls adorning her neck. The isolation of this fragment by LakeVerea also interrogates female representation under the male gaze marked by an asymmetric morality: is she really laughing? Social contrasts, which have marked the national landscape more than *mestizaje*, are also a concern for the artists. Other of their photographs capture slogans by the Mexican Communist Party that appear in Diego Rivera's mural *El hombre controlador del universo* (1933), originally a commission for the Rockefeller Center that was destroyed and then remade for Bellas Artes: "We want work not charity"; "Divided we starve, united we eat, we can't eat blue birds." Images of the slogans hang across from *Candil de cristal*, which portrays one of the three gigantic art deco chandeliers hanging at the Sala Nacional at the Palace, designed in Paris by Edgar Brandt. The juxtaposition of a luxurious element from the environment inhabited by the class in power contrasting with the workers' slogans from Rivera's murals conveys a counternarrative to Mexican modernist nationalism grounded on *mestizaje* and inclusion.

The photograph titled *A la verdad le falta el espejo, sostiene sólo el mango* (Truth is lacking a mirror, she is only holding the handle) registers a fragment from a sculpture from the main façade of the Palace. In my reading,

FIGURE 4. LakeVerea, *A la verdad le falta el espejo* (2019; The truth is missing the mirror), from the exhibition *LakeVerea vs. Bellas Artes*, © LakeVerea.

the image is directly allusive to the current politico-cultural situation. The image of the sculpture was "edited" by the artists to offer us a faceless figure covered in a light cloth that barely allows us to see her legs and veiled sex. What good is a handle without a mirror, the mirror being the site where the truth becomes visible?

LakeVerea's exhibition inaugurates an era in which a need for crypto-graphic, cypherpunk, and nonelitist art is needed, in a context in which public space is transparent yet intolerant to critique that is showing through innocuous passions. Because power is rejecting and dismissing direct criti-cism, it has become necessary to disseminate private and cyphered mes-sages of resistance. In this case: to contest the legitimation of the nation and heteropatriachy through the monumentality of public national architecture.

The Preprogrammed State of Being Happy

Our heteropatriarchal capitalist society's mandate to search for a "good life" is definitely an amalgam of fantasy, negation, and futility, because the main mediators of human relationships are fear and the market. Therefore, as for Sisyphus, the constant search for happiness makes us bump into a wall made up of our frustrated desires, because the possibility of satisfying what we believe are our needs is thwarted by capitalism. The system not only interpellates individuals manipulating our libido but creates desiring subjectivities that will never be satisfied by consumption and that remain trapped in a Sisyphean loop of endless stimulation. In parallel, a new science has been developed: "positive psychology." Its supreme end is to achieve happiness through a combination of psychological work and personal growth. Edgar Cabanas and Eva Illouz drew a genealogy of this science.[1] According to their analysis, happiness and the individual capacity for self-determination are indistinguishable, and their goal is personal self-realization. The tools to achieve this are self-help, positive emotions, happiness, and learnt optimism. This new sensibility is grounded on the scientific study of human well-being and happiness and is applied by corporations to augment productivity, diminish work-related stress, and to promote employees' engagement with the company. Self-help and the science of happiness also serve to optimize the self through *coaching* tailored to every pocket: from the Pentecostal Church, which is free, all the way up to sects for the 1 percent, like Keith Rainiere's *NXVIUM* (dismantled due to sexual and financial scandals in 2019).

In spite of the general decline in quality of life and opportunities for economic progress, the technocratic concept of "happiness" is measured objectively and universally by life-expectancy, social policies, freedom, and income. According to the Worldwide Happiness report of the United Nations of 2019, the happiest countries in the world are Finland, Denmark, and Norway for the quality of education, healthcare system, life expectancy, GDP, freedom, and social aid they offer. Mexico ranks number twenty-three on the world happiness indexes. Without a doubt, learned optimism fosters the growth of the individualist, technocratic, and utilitarian soul, but if we remember that fear is the main mediator of inter-collective relationships, frustration and impotence, along with anxiety and depression epidemics, are at the root of interpersonal relationships. In a way, the futile search for a destiny of unreachable happiness is linked to a general state of affairs that is unstable and precarious. In the process of finding individual happiness, we are hindered in seeing the larger picture that is directly affecting our quality of life. What possibilities for true solidarity exist in this context of emotional and work instability, in an endless search for individual self-realization? The limits drawn between bodies are now being drawn by digital communication, by the ubiquity of images when we make ourselves present to each other through our own representation in social media, by the distribution of bodies by urban planning, through collective exhaustion, by excess of work and responsibility, indifference, disillusionment, and the fear of others. The only thing that we share is the toxicity of our own atmosphere. What chances are there to recognize and be-with, of communion?

Crisis of Relationality
and Being/Having

Félix Guattari diagnosed a crisis of relationality at the end of the 1980s and describes it in the following manner:

> The Earth is undergoing a period of intense techno-scientific transforma-
> tions. If no remedy is found, the ecological disequilibrium this has gener-
> ated will ultimately threaten the continuation of life on the planet's surface.
> Alongside these upheavals, human modes of life, both individual and collec-
> tive, are progressively deteriorating. Kinship networks tend to be reduced to
> a bare minimum; domestic life is being poisoned by the gangrene of mass
> media consumption; family and married life are frequently "ossified" by a
> sort of standardization of behavior; and neighborhood relations are gener-
> ally reduced to their meanest expression. . . . It is the relationship between
> subjectivity and its exteriority—be it social, animal, vegetable or Cosmic—
> that is comprised in this way, in a sort of general movement of implosion
> and regressive infantilization.[1]

This crisis of relationality has been exacerbated by the implementation of neoliberal policies and the advent of digital technologies, and almost no one has been able to understand the implications of this crisis. Franco Berardi has compared our neoliberal society to a state of social interaction in prison: in comradeship under such circumstances, empathy is vacuous and solidarity impossible.[2] While our bodies are exhausted and depressed, our capacity for attention—in general and toward others—diminishes radically; in our narcissistic and hyperconsumerist society, the world presents itself to us

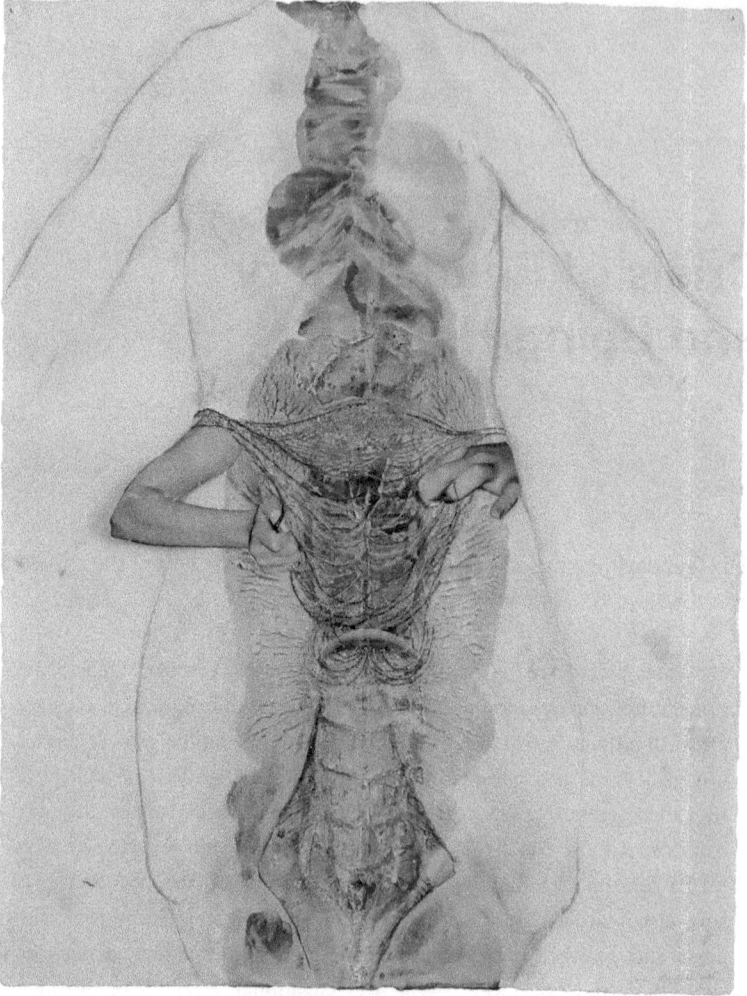

FIGURE 5. Valérie Mannaerts, *Verveuse* (1999), drawing and collage on paper, 65 × 50 cm, courtesy of the artist.

as projections of the I, diluting even more the limits between the I and the other. Internal experience becomes the constant need to make oneself present to everyone (in social media, for instance) but without having any responsibility toward others; internal experience is also translated to being tied to nothing except to the corporate powers that connect everything and everyone else. The Catholic Church attempted to get rid of the human libido for two thousand years and finally capitalism completed this mission: the last half century of permissiveness, sexual liberation, pornography, and consumerism led capitalism and technology to capture our desires, teaching us how to disconnect our bodies from our psyches, our desires from the other, reducing humans to eternally stimulated beings who can never achieve orgasm or satisfaction. We are trying to fill the void left by permanent sensual dissatisfaction and alienation with monogamy as an untouchable family structure that is continuously falling apart, and by "helicopter parenting," living vicariously through our children and their successes.

Under the situation of the crisis of relationality, violence has become an instrument to propagate the toxicity of the obstinate rigidity of codes and desires imposed by the heteropatriarchal capitalist regime. Those codes and desires translate to processes through which human bodies are constituted as sovereign according to a hierarchy in which some win the right to live or die, to produce or reproduce; a few have access to the market as consumers/workers, but most are denied access; all are molded by the pharmacopornographic regime, which reproduces artificial femininity and masculinity with chemicals and images, the latter maintaining psyches in an eternal cycle of excitation-frustration.

The bodies that have access to production and consumption processes are inserted as "people-within-society" with a market position in the "new-individuals-economy." While all your identification documents (CURP, IFE, RFC) are linked to your cell phone, credit card, your Instagram, Facebook, Bank, Netflix, Uber, Tinder, Waze, WhatsApp accounts, you begin to leave traces everywhere, becoming data and thus a source of capital. The virtual "you" that is formed is trapped in the guts of the globalized network of virtual infrastructure in which "your" individual characteristics, "your" health, "your" sense of humor, "your" physical appearance, "your" skills, "your" social relations, and "your" education level, creative capacities, consumption choices, and political ideas are interpreted as data: the most valuable asset in today's globalized economy. You have no other choice but to follow the mandate of working and exploiting yourself; you look your best, especially in Instagram; you drink lots of wine, vape pot at social events, you allow the guy above you in your work hierarchy to grab your boob and remain silent; you have children, you empower yourself but try not to shine more than your (male) partner; you repeat what you hear on the radio and read in important newspapers by noted opinion-makers, being careful that your opinion follows strictly the main line of governmental institutions and commentators that belong to the same class as do you; above all, you defend them; you have chosen a profession that is appropriate for "women"; you find ways of existing that would never threaten men, especially sexually; you try to be neat and make a lot of money while making sure people know you share your money with others, because your respectability as a person is now measured after the number of *likes* your posts gather. In all these ways, institutions exist within you while the past encroaches on the future, making time, reality, and humans dislocated from each other.

The internalization of institutions has also dislocated our perception of the world from bodily experience: we tend to perceive reality through signs manifest as external referents—the only referents embedded in our memories. That is to say, bodily experience is superseded by experiences codified in external reality, and that is the reason why it is so difficult to truly connect with people. If we explain this form of dissociation through the filter of the sensorium of violence, we could state that violence has to do with the borders between the I—and predictably—the hierarchical distribution of sovereignty on bodies.

If people, time, and reality are all out of joint, it is because the I is permanently dislocated and disjointed from the body, along with subjective knowledge, personal belief, and collective knowledge—or common sense. That is why the lesson the *killjoys* teach us is to make sense of what does not make sense, interrupting and resisting the structures that maintain the status quo and keep women silenced. To be a *killjoy* implies to be at war with the fury we bear inside,[3] although we may be accused of not knowing how to control our own emotions. Because while emotions can be worked on, and might subside once we verbalize them, in truth they get stuck in between the layers of the lower back muscles and if that is not worked on, we are permanently uncomfortable in the long term: it is easy to see it in women older than seventy who traverse physical space with difficulty. And because, as Kathy Acker says, emotion moves more slowly and tyrannically than thought,[4] it is very difficult to get rid of emotions generated by the sensorium of violence. And violence is within ourselves because we are taught to internalize it since childhood, to normalize it, to accept it:

> her mom did not teach her how to accept a lover's caress, a kind word, or a helping hand. so instead we did shots of jameson and fucked every friday night in a bathroom stall in bar down the road by a lake, not too far from here. that's how we were gentle.[5]

The impossibility of receiving and giving love is rooted here in the maternal impossibility of having given and taught love, giving leeway to a chain of un-love and abuse rooted in colonialism and heteropatriarchy that spreads vertically, from generation to generation, and horizontally, across the relational field.

Abusive Love

On April 2016 I saw flourish on my Facebook wall an endless collection of confessions and accusations from women encouraged by the question asked by Colombian activist and columnist Catalina Ruiz Navarro: "When was the first time you were *acosada* (stalked/abused/harassed)?" In the context of the National Day of Mobilization against Machista Violence, and trying to overcome the status of victims, the collective denunciation—which soon became massive—was lived as an act of courage and empowerment and as a step forward to prevent future gender violence. This campaign preceded the globally known #MeToo movement launched in Hollywood in 2017. Surprise, indignation—also relief—have spread now that we know how common abuse in all its nuances is, from unwanted catcalling, to subtle forms of coercion like unexpected grabs, to rape and femicide. We instituted a space and a vocabulary to speak about forms of abuse. The fact that there is a "first time" that almost every woman remembers attests to the fact that gender violence is a means of heteropatriarchal subjectivation (or "a pedagogy") that prepares girls and young women to keep on being abused throughout their lives and to invisibilize the abuse. The #MiPrimerAcoso campaign was followed by another one initiated in March 2019 to directly denounce abuses of power in work relations and in the intellectual and academic realms. Twitter hashtags were established—#MeTooEscritoras (writers), #MeTooArtes (arts), #MeTooAcademia, #MeTooCine (film), and so on—to disseminate concrete cases and the names of abusers, causing upheaval in social media.

In this context, feminist activist and intellectual Marta Lamas questioned the fact that the signifier "abuse" has been used to describe an array of behaviors: from harassment by someone in a higher hierarchical position at work, school, or home; to acts in public spaces perpetrated by unknown men making unseemly propositions, calling out names or whistling to women; to unwanted and nonconsensual touching and rape. What concerns Lamas is the punitive attitude that has been taken as a measure to eradicate and prevent "abuse" and the new form of sexual puritanism and fear that came with the denunciations of abuse.[1] Clearly, the call to denounce and put a stop to abuse is a scream that goes beyond denouncing and ending inequality, double standards, and machismo. According to Lamas, however, many of the behaviors, attitudes, and actions denunciated have been part of the customs and habits generated by cultural gender mandates that define what is "proper" to men, which is to conquer women. And what is "proper" to women in this context is not only to manifest disinterest or disdain toward men's proposals but also to never express desire of any kind, especially sexual. This is how abusive masculine, machista behavior was normalized in our society. This behavior needs to be eradicated, but it is not comparable to sexual abuse or femicide. According to Lamas, moreover, we must draw a distinction between harassment and abuse and quid pro quo practices, a form of instrumental sexuality which implies that "I sleep with you because I want something in exchange"; this behavior must be distinguished from expressive sexuality: "I am having sex with you because I desire you." For Lamas, it is important to consider that the use of sexual capital to obtain something in return (in the context, for instance, of Hollywood actresses who denounced pressure to give sexual favors to Harvey Weinstein to obtain privileges) is not necessarily abuse. What is problematic, and what drove women to denounce these kinds of situations, is a manifest power imbalance in work relationships and the clear differentiation of social privileges between men and women. What we must bear in mind, according to Lamas, is that in our struggle to emancipate ourselves from heteropatriarchy, we must be careful not to fall into puritanism or to posit harassment as a crime and punish it. Rather, we need to launch a collective enterprise of pedagogy and resubjectivation, a "cognitive emancipation" according to Paul B. Preciado.[2]

When awareness of the magnitude of the problem that is suffered (or survived) individually by most women became tangible, something shook our society to the core. The conclusion is that most women live through traumatic sexual experiences. Beyond the fact that the public denunciation of abuse could lead to killing the possibility of seduction games, or that we are a society that has failed to recognize, or rather has systemically invisibilized, gender violence, what is at the root of all forms of abuse is that since birth women have been coerced into being compliant, to never say no. Once the gender mandate of femininity has been internalized, females

are conditioned to naturalize an imposed docility that prepares us for subjection, hinders us from naming the act of aggression, confuses anger and
shame with the apparent incapacity to control our own emotions and bodies. But it also has to do with something much more deep that is rooted in
our societies: normalization of abuse as a form of love.

For bell hooks, abuse and neglect are opposed to care and sustenance, but
most of us come from dysfunctional families in which we have been verbally
or physically abused and emotionally neglected.[3] In extreme cases, aggression and humiliation coexist with gestures of love and care, and thus as children we learn that abuse is an expression of love, shaping the way we perceive
love as adults. Disbelief also comes from the shadiness of abuse, because it
is cornered between pleasure and taboo, transgression and empowerment,
damage and liberation. Eimear McBride's *A Girl Is a Half-Formed Thing*
(2015) deals with this, as does Veronica Gonzalez's *The Sad Passions*, from
which I'm copying and cutting a passage for you to read:

> Who were they? But that they were older, I am sure. I remember once on the
> bed, rolling around, maybe they were touching us then? I don't know, though
> I imagine they were because I do have a strong sense of my skin going all hot
> where they touched me, on my crotch, and we were giggling and their hands
> were on, or maybe even in our panties—the squirming away and then being
> caught. A strange form of tag. Like little dogs. Trying to crawl away on all
> fours and then being pulled back by our legs, our shriek laughter.
>
> We were doing this, moving like this, in this, crawling and shrieking and
> laughing and being grabbed and pulling away and being grabbed and get-
> ting pulled back and then being grabbed again, and there was nothing
> strange in it, nothing wrong in it, we felt, until Grandma Marina's tenant,
> a middle-aged woman, maybe ten years older than our mother, ten years
> older than Claudia, until this woman descended the stairs outside the big
> window; and when she glanced in, she saw. . . .
>
> The boys were older, Her eyes made me see that. . . . Her eyes . . . which
> to me seemed tinged with shame and sadness. . . . And then I never again,
> until Julian, let a boy touch me like that.[4]

The story told by Veronica is about a Mexican family narrated from the
points of view of six women that live around Cecilia, who suffers from depression and mental illness perhaps as a result of gender violence. Cecilia's
daughters tell their own stories from the points of view of their childhood,

teenage years, and early adulthood. Verónica's description of the teenagers' coming of age is traversed by the dangers and damage of gender violence and vulnerability due to intergenerational trauma. The descriptions of the relationships between the sisters and the rest of the family are especially moving and insightful and touch upon something Mississauga Nishnaabeg writer, musician, and academic Leanne Betamosake Simpson has also tried to describe: how vulnerability to gender violence is somehow inherited from mother to daughter and then keeps on spreading everywhere, to the edges between me and others, actually giving shape to gender and to gender relations.

While I seek out strategies to appease my anger and aggression, like writing and training, I worry about my ten-year-old. How do I prepare her for the fact that it is likely that she or someone she deeply cares about will be at some point abused? Exacerbated by "necro-empowerment" and the loss of value of life, in a place where femicide is common and impunity is the rule? In these neofascist and polarized times, I think it is urgent to find bases in common for a feminism that can resist the temptation to pluralize struggles grounded on gender identity, ethnicity, sexual preference. Because gender violence goes beyond these distinctions we have drawn to empower ourselves. I think it is urgent to flip around the slogan "the private is personal and thus political" into "I take personally the political that is a collective problem."

Water Running under
the Bridge

When you asked me why I felt torn when I decided to stop seeing the Artist, the answer I could give you at the time was extremely vague and left you even more confused on the subject. But you do know I need to write to figure things out for myself. In retrospect, it was very disappointing to realize that the story was nothing other than a vulgar repetition of an ego and power game based on the asymmetry of privileges created by gender difference that operates in almost all realms in which we circulate. Somehow, I suspect that he had felt threatened by me and decided to do something about it. As you know, that story began with a critical text I wrote about an artwork by the Artist, a piece that I found profoundly problematic for first, instrumentalizing art, putting into practice a social program that I saw as profoundly condescending—verging on populism—and with the end of inciting the participants to join the cycle of consumption as a solution to violence. Second, because his artistic intervention (which was carried out in many cities in the country and abroad), is akin to a certain neoliberal logic inherent to public policy that falsely promotes citizen participation in the name of "social art," promoting a temporary solution to a long-term problem as opposed to change.

Without personally knowing the Artist or having sought to carry out a personal attack against him or his work, a few months after I published the text on my blog, in a second article I questioned some of the premises inherent to another of his pieces then exhibited at a local museum. I felt that the message transmitted by the second piece carried the same problematic neoliberal values as the other, that is to say, an apolitical sensibility produced by the junction of liberal with utilitarian and capitalist values. I also sensed that the Artist's obvious lack of political position, which characterizes much of his work, is also part of the "ideological" of our era: the production of apparently politicized artworks that reaffirm the neoliberal principles of democratic participation and freedom of expression while praising technology and nationalist narratives. That is to say, cultural power tends to promote cultural expressions that invisibilize dispossession and the destruction of the redundant populations and their life-forms by extractivism and financial capitalism. The second text I wrote about the Artist had been commissioned by an editor to be published in a well-known art criticism magazine that came out in print and online. A short time after it was published, however, the text was mysteriously erased from the website; when I inquired about the absence of the text, the editor vehemently affirmed that there had been an unsolvable problem with the server. The text did not completely disappear because it circulated in print and I posted it on my blog (as I do every time I am censored: the blog has now become a profuse *salon des refusés*). A short time after the text's disappearance from the art criticism magazine online, the Artist got in touch with me to establish a dialogue and a friendship. I would later understand his gesture as a crusade to persuade me to stop writing "negative critique" about his work. When we met in person, he noted that artists are accustomed now to only read laudatory texts about their work in exhibition catalogues and reviews. And it might be the case, that the genre of art criticism is a casualty of the culture industry.

As you do know the story well, his intentions of making friends soon became direct seduction (including giving me films and books as gifts). I fell for it. An intense affair followed that lasted a few months, which he ended to supposedly protect his marriage, painted by him to me as a coexistence agreement based on an "open" relationship. During the months that followed, we tried to transform the intense sexual and affective relationship into friendship and dialogue (or at least I tried), which we achieved to a point, collaborating in two small projects. This is when you came into my life and I felt immensely lucky to have found someone I could love with all my strength, someone with whom I could have something more intense and important than what the stupid previous affair had given me. I suppose that I had fallen into the classic trap of reacting emotionally and affectively to the situation of being confronted by the Artist whose work I had criticized, which he then instrumentalized to exercise manipulating power, appearing and reappearing, initiating the affair one last time . . . until he made sure "our friendship" was more important to me than art criticism (I suppose).

Because I had indeed agreed to eliminate the first text I had written from one of the chapters on a forthcoming book and the second text from my blog for the sake of "friendship." That is when I made the conscious decision to be open to his aesthetic-political position, as opposed to interrogating it. I even invited the Artist to my art theory class so we could have a discussion in front of my students, a space that the Artist unfortunately seized not to discuss our disagreements, but to reaffirm and preach his position. I let him, even feeling a bit guilty.

Every time that I thought I was establishing an intellectual and political dialogue with the Artist—based obviously on uncomfortable disagreements—I sensed that our conversations were not fruitful, almost empty, we were getting nowhere. It was never a true dialogue but a space in which the Artist tried to justify himself, his work, his life project. He also challenged me to abandon theory and criticism—in his view futile because they don't propose solutions, only negativity, according to him—and to get hands-on in political action. He insisted so much in the pragmatism of concrete solutions, the futility of critical thinking, that I don't think for him, or even maybe in this society, there is place for idealism: only results and profits, like in business. At the end I realized that he couldn't care less about my ideas and that whatever I could bring to the table to enrich his practice was beyond his radar. Another disappointing moment was when he pompously offered me a damaged copy of his recently published *catalogue raisonné* that I immediately rejected, demanding a good copy.

In retrospect, my attempts to establish a relationship of intellectual dialogue and friendship covered a need to heal my pride, of putting to the side the emotional damage the affair had caused me (I had a major heartbreak) and above all, the silencing and self-censorship that his "friendship" had cost me.

I sat down for a last coffee with the Artist at El Olvidado in Coyoacán. That week, scandals of sexual harassment and abuse in Europe and in the US were unleashed by the artworld version of the #MeToo campaign. A prestigious curator in New York had been fired, the accusation had destroyed his personal life and career; similar accusations had begun to resonate against powerful men in the artworld mostly in the North. In this last conversation, the Artist made a strange declaration that I understood as both an awkward confession and apology: "I will never behave like that, nothing like what happened between us will happen again." I felt panic and . . .false shame? In the tone of his voice. Then I thought about the young foreign curator who had told me that months earlier that the Artist had tried to seduce her on an Uber ride, putting his hand on her leg (not long after our affair). She was profoundly disgusted and offended. I had said nothing, only "Ew!" I left El Olvidado on a terrible mood, on high guard and ready to confront my own negation.

Sometimes after our encounters, the Artist would give me or lend me books and that time, I left with a good pile he'd given me as loans or gifts. That day he had made a strange selection from his library to give me: Adam Weiner's *How Bad Writing Destroyed the World* and a book about women's testimonies in Mexican jails. They weren't necessarily titles I had shown interest in, and I received them as farewell gifts and warnings. The scene from Godard's *Une femme est une femme* (1961) in which the couple argues by showing each other titles of books, letting them take the place of enunciations or accusations, came to my mind. Ironically, *How Bad Writing Destroyed the World* is a book that connects the individualist and objectivist philosophy of rationalist selfishness behind Ayn Rand's books (one of the topics of our discussions) with the radical ethics of destruction inherent to the current neoliberal system.

I am angry for agreeing willingly!!! to have censored myself, while I acknowledge my responsibility in having taken part in the story. The ambiguity that there can be in relationships between men and women, however, is deepened because the artworld lends itself to transgression and experimentation with nonnormative practices like polyamorousness (see Gabriela Wiener's confessional writing). The artworld, however, is perfectly divided into heteropatriarchal gender roles: women translate (through criticism and curating), manage, and finance (as directors or gallerists) the production of male artists. Indeed for the most part, women are in charge of the reproductive work in the culture field as managers and guardians of the patrimony, while men play the role of creators and producers of discourses and artworks. Obviously, this division of roles grants men more privileges and power not only in the artworld, but in the world in general.

To address these issues doesn't mean to victimize women for emotional or physical violence exercised against us by men: we are very far from being characters from an Elena Garro novel, lost and aimless in the world with few tools to survive, ending up being destroyed by the men upon whom they depend or by their circumstances of being alone without a man (I get chills just thinking that Garro's novels have autobiographical traits). And although the world Elena Garro describes in her novels is gone, traces of it remain in our social relationships. Not long ago, I heard an adult man tearing apart a twenty-something-year-old woman artist who is extremely talented: "If she looked more after herself and cared for her appearance . . . her face is too big and angular, she is overweight, she lacks self-confidence. Her work is a farce because she is a millionaire bourgeois kid who believes she is a communist.

FIGURE 6. Magali Lara, photo by Nicolás Echeverría, courtesy of the artist.

She has a parasite boyfriend sucking her blood and money . . ." When men allow themselves such great misogyny, they are normalizing the positioning of women as vulnerable to gender violence. This is why canceling an abuser has become a resource for attempting to get rid of the problem at the root, and sometimes just pointing a finger at the person is enough.

Clearly, these kinds of situations and behaviors are perpetuated by the privileges heteropatriarchy gives men and also because women remain silent. That is why, some time ago, many women signed a letter that circulated in the artworld in Spanish. We wanted to establish a mechanism of denunciation—a virtual *tendedero*—without necessarily ending artists' careers (and means of family sustenance) or falling into calumny and jealousy. Circulating the list of predatory men was a means to look after each other. The practice of cancellation, akin to public lynching, is extremely dangerous, as attempts to legally solve cases of abuse and harassment have resulted in the accused, instead of apologizing and promising to change, going to lawyers who recommend they deny the charges: negation becomes an instance of salvation. Another of the questions that is being asked is if we can separate the "man" from his actions and work or not?

PS: I am reading Rita Macedo's memoir, written and compiled by her daughter Cecilia Fuentes. The pattern of misogynous behavior of "geniuses" (or cultural agents) is very clearly spelled out there. Imagine! Macedo recalls the suicide of at least eight "princesses" (women Carlos Fuentes had affairs with, while married to her). Mind you, Macedo killed herself some years after Fuentes left her. She was a talented actor and visionary film and theater producer who devoted all her energies to Fuentes' career while they were together.

And Water Not Running

Some time ago, four women got together to sign and disseminate in social media a public declaration stating they would cease working with TE, a curator and writer living in X against whom they made serious accusations. The women either had had intimate or working relationships with him linked to publishing or organizing art exhibitions. They denounced him for his abusive behavior, for making them undergo his modus operandi, which they described as a pattern of manipulative and abusive behavior across four continents. They also accused him of being a "serial predator," for using their prestige as a platform to collaborate with women and nonbinary people, most of them younger or in more vulnerable positions than his, to establish intimate relationships that led to theft of their creative and intellectual labor. For them, TE kept on expanding his "hunting grounds" through professional networks that his victims also belonged to. That is why the four (serious, prestigious professional) women signing the public declaration put pressure on the members of their networks to cut professional ties with this "deeply toxic person." With their declaration, the women sought to stop TE from continuing to abuse women and the LGBTQI+ community. Finally, they declared that they would not take part in any event, book, or project if TE was involved.

TE happens to be an old friend and colleague, and the news of the public declaration did not surprise me: I believe the four denouncers. TE, however, never manifested to me his "predator" side, I always felt respected by him, he treated me as a colleague and good friend. And although once he tried to approach me sexually, his approximation was soft and my rejection did not affect our friendship. And I repeat, I don't have any doubt that TE has a predatory side linked to his exacerbated ambition. He always gave me the impression that—as any ambitious person—TE would be capable of doing anything good or bad to achieve his goals, even and in spite of declaring himself to be a feminist, polyamorous, and submissive. Maybe he did so to capitalize on his masculine privilege. Being able to put myself on the side of his abusers and believing them, though, I find myself before a dilemma. I don't believe in the professional and social murder of anyone. To me, it is a simplistic solution that reduces the problem to isolated cases of abuse and falls short in being able to undo prevailing and self-reproducing hetero-patriarchal patterns of abuse. Underlying the cancellation of abusers are daily micro-misogynies expanded throughout the social field that remain silenced, as do the structures that maintain men in positions of privilege— for instance, the gendered division of productive and reproductive work. How could we turn around the negativity of cancellation that is imposed as a solution to misogynistic predation? Part of the problem is that in our neofascist era, the defense and visibilization of victims' ordeals of racism, classism, and misogyny has become a kind of morality that now triggers all human action. The problem is that this morality comes with absolute negativity and without redemption, leading to a form of pervasive fascism grounded on the remnants of liberal values, in as far as our adherence to or rejection of them is what marks the deep and violent polarizations that characterize our present.

For instance, a story by the *Guardian* informs that two militants in favor of meat consumption protested in front of a vegan supermarket in London by eating raw chipmunks still covered in skin.[1] The men were arrested for disturbing public order, but they defended themselves by stating that they were against veganism and that by eating raw chipmunks in public, they sought to create consciousness about the dangers of ceasing to ingest animal protein. For their action, they were wearing shirts with the legend: "Veganism = malnutrition." Although passersby and shoppers begged them to stop eating the chipmunks because they caused disgust, they refused to. The violence inherent to this anti-vegan act is akin to the social and professional witch hunt against abusers. The anti-vegan act is an example of the form that the fascism bred from liberal values is taking, in the sense of stigmatization and cancellation of the other as a solution to their immorality. That goes with a new puritanism grounded on sexual panic that Marta Lamas warns us against.

I am not vouching for TE or defending him or anyone else who has abused or harassed one or many women. What I want to put on the table is the possibility of an affirmative politics that could lead us to imagine—at the political, not ethical, level—social horizons of hope for a posthetero-

patriarchal society. But first and foremost, before abandoning critical negativity, we need to resist moralistic, fascistic puritan negativity that reduces
misogyny and abuse to immorality or aberration that can be corrected by
cancellation.

In political terms, the precondition to ending heteropatriarchal misogyny
would be to reject the conditions that facilitate abusive or unfair practices,
then to give way to a cognitive and epistemological change in how we live
with gender difference. Instead of pointing a finger at a person or at a case,
to certain victims, we need to detect patterns of behavior that are generally
accepted in our societies but that are toxic and come to mediate peoples'
relationships. The patterns that generate abuse, moreover, do not necessarily come from sexual difference, but from a culture of upbringing and
the families in which we were educated.

The central theme of the Apple series *The Morning Show* (2019) is the
way patterns of abuse work in the microcosm of a daily morning show on
a prestigious TV network in the US. The host of the program, Mitch Kes-
sler (Steve Carell), is anonymously accused of abusing a woman, and the
network's director fires him from the show. His co-host, Alex Levy (Jennifer
Aniston), invites garrulous and engaged journalist Bradley Jackson (Reese
Witherspoon) to be her new partner on the morning show. The three characters get wrapped up in a network of tensions interwoven through the
mechanisms of veiling and unveiling other cases of abuse within the chain.

Mitch's is not an isolated case or incident, but one of the "uses and customs" of the network's culture that perpetuate and silence abusive kinds of
behavior. The story reveals the complicities and power games that sustain
the benevolence of women regarding their colleagues' abuse of masculine
privileges.

In a chapter from his most recent book of chronicles, *Ahora imagino
cosas* (2019), Julián Herbert discusses the murder of a young poor woman
in Chile alongside the narration of a discussion between four male writers
sitting at a table drinking and talking about a #MeToo accusation amongst
the Chilean writer's community. "Le cayó un *me too*," is the phrase one
of them uses, writes Herbert: "A *me too* fell upon him, as if those things
grew up on trees and suddenly landed on someone's lap, like poisoned fruit,
poetry is an uncomfortable cherry."[2] Herbert says he believes her, but he
likes the accused's writing, and goes on to declare that his opinion on the
matter of the *me too*s is that he observes a generational fissure between
Anglo-Saxon and Latin American thinkers in their fifties and sixties and
the younger generation on the matter. Avoiding discussing the matter concretely, he moves on to elucidate whether he is entitled or has the moral

right to write about the femicide of a young working class woman (as he shares her background), or whether a middle-class woman who has been raped by a writer colleague is more entitled than him to write about the topic. He moves on to declare that "the female body is a powerful metonymy and the price they have to pay for it is high."[3] Before going to bed, he writes, he decides to watch reruns of *MILF* and *Bar de Chicas*, two Chilean shows about, with, and for women. Throughout the entire text, Herbert meanders through instances of gender violence, dodging taking a stand or any responsibility while resisting giving a male point of view about femicide, abuse, the #MeToo movement, or male privilege. Perhaps in an attempt to be provocative and disguise his own silent complicity with the matter, he keeps on repeating, "poetry is a rotten cherry."

Vanessa Springora's memoir of her affair when she was thirteen with writer Gabriel Matzneff are as devastating as Siri Hustvedt's novel *The Blazing World* (2014) is angering. Decades after her affair with Matzneff, Springora had the courage to write about her love story and the destructive sequels of self-harm and emotional damage it left behind. What surprises the narrator, over and over again, is that when she was together with Matzneff, adults around her were tolerant of it, perhaps, she speculates, because the 1970s were permissive and lived under the mandate that everyone (including children) had to free themselves from sexual repression. The title of Springora's book, *Consent*, interrogates the meaning of taking part in a relationship in which there is a deep power and experience asymmetry, and there is also a huge difference in both person's capacity to manipulate the other. Springora recalls in one passage a visit she makes to the existentialist philosopher Émile Cioran, which alludes to Herbert's "rotten cherry" that justifies the misogyny of "geniuses." Vanessa goes to see Cioran looking for answers about her affair with Matzneff: "G. is an artist, a great writer . . . you love him and you must accept his personality. G. will never change. It is an immense honor he has chosen you. Your role is to accompany him on the road of creation and you must also comply to all of his whims . . . often women can't understand what an artist needs . . . the love that a woman in love with an artist must confer upon her beloved needs to be sacrificial and self-obliterating." Vanessa answered, "But Émile, he lies to me all the time," to which Cioran responds, "Lies are literature, dear friend."[4]

When we come to understand that what we call "abuse," in the sense of unwanted sexual approaches or touching and quid pro quo practices due to the generalized power imbalance relationships in gender divisions that sustain heteropatriarchy, is something systemic and tolerated by the whole of society as opposed to isolated scandalous cases, we will realize that it is urgent to find forms of becoming that are empowering not only for women but for all of society. These forms of empowerment will not come from achieving the social and professional death of a person, as toxic as he or she may be. So the change in perspective I am proposing is based on the political ideal of augmenting our capacities to relate to multiple others, cultivating relationships that can lead us to reject and transform our own toxic values and to rethink women's sexual freedom not as a puritan retreat from masculine "objectification" but as the right to play with self-objectification, offering and retiring as one wishes, acknowledging that sexuality is indeed traversed by power games and obscenities.

Vulnerability

By slowly becoming everything.
—Arundhati Roy[1]

How did we get to live in a world where destroying lives is an instrument for necro-empowerment and bodies are not only merchandise (as in the times of legal slavery), but disposable instruments vulnerable to all kinds of violence? The contemporary absolute lack of empathy for others reminds us of worldwide indifference before the extermination of Europe's Jews and contrasts with our contemporary civil society's notion of charity—for instance, protecting abandoned or stray dogs. The number of private organizations just in Mexico City that recue pets is surprising, especially if we put this phenomenon in the context of entire populations across the country and traversing the territory being systematically displaced, disappeared, violated, barely surviving. How can we understand these two simultaneous phenomena? I want to attribute the origin of the current crisis of empathy not only to hypercompetitiveness at work, which transforms the other, the neighbor, the friend into the enemy, or to racism capable of undoing the other to the point of literal obliteration. Perhaps the crisis of empathy is tied to the general condition of being detached from each other and to our cultivated capacity to dissociate from our bodies and from everything else surrounding us.

Numbed within and without, we have come to believe that our self-worth derives from this irrational feeling of self-reliance, perhaps nurtured by our mothers since birth.[2] An example of this could be the Ferber method that "teaches" babies to self-soothe by letting them cry themselves to sleep in their crib. This early programming to self-rely is accompanied by a conception of the body as a rational machine. Obliged to repress our own vulnerability, we become detached from our bodies, each other, and the world. This phenomenon can be thought a parallel to the Western ideal of a search for totality, premised on a fictitious unity of the subject. But somewhat I suspect that subjectivity is always already fragmented and dislocated, and that the fragments get shattered by these series of constitutive separations and incessant dislocations, which includes the pain of not being rooted on earth and of communal dismemberment. These originary shatterings are linked to Western modernity, presupposed on a denial of what Jean-Luc Nancy calls the "being-with" of the ontology of being.[3] There are two myths that dissimulate the reality of such fragmentation: that the I can be completed by overcoming the fractures or by following the platonic ideal of love, finding her twin soul. Although we do live by the ideals that a self is or can become whole by overcoming brokenness or finding love, some chose to believe in the fracture, on the self-dismemberment or on shattering subjectivity as being potentially emancipatory. "No pain, no gain!" said the 1980s slogan that we repeated to ourselves in the collective furor for frantically exercising. In radical queer acts of social, psychic, and epistemological disruption, queering means to shatter "normal" or given gender identities and to erect communities with impermanent links without the promise of a new sociality or identity. If queer means to shatter hegemonic forms of sociality, vanguard artists experimented with the shattering of the I in different ways: through sexuality, the use of substances that alter perception, living outside of the norm. I can think of Pita Amor, Nahui Ollin, Frida Kahlo, Kathy Acker, Virginie Despentes. But what does it mean to self-liquefy when a self is already shattered, when the violence of gender and gender violence are forms of shattering subjection in themselves, the famous "constitutive wound"? What is freedom or liberation from this perspective?[4]

I propose that instead of self-liquefying further, we learn to embrace our own fractures, shatterings, vulnerability. I'm not thinking about *subjectification*, which implies taking a textual position, cultural appropriation, or even political positioning; neither is embracing vulnerability about *subjectification* in the sense of reinventing oneself in a mix of a libidinal drive and the neoliberal mandate to find ways to adapt and stay competitive in the market. When I think about what it would mean to come to terms with the fragmentation of our own being, recognizing the violent practices of subjectivation that constitute us, I am reminded of this recipe that I heard once: when a tool is damaged to the point it can no longer be used, it needs to burn red-hot and then be smoothed out so the damaged part can be removed by submerging it in water. This water can be drunk—you should actually drink the story of the damage and the repair; with faith, you can even heal the source of the damage. Afterward, you may give the broken part a new function or purpose. While this recipe is for repairing iron tools, healing by "drinking the story" and repurposing the damaged part might work as a strategy to embrace our own shattering, through a sort of cathartic separation from the damaged part, cleansing, and then communing with the remains. So vulnerability could become the capacity to accept a state of pain or insecurity, submitting or delivering the self to the feeling of coming undone.

But what does it actually mean to be vulnerable and not embrace it? I feel it's something I've tried to hide from others and from myself. At the cost of headaches, IBS and leaky gut, a wrecked immune system, the inability of articulating a sentence. A mental-physical feeling of paralysis. I suspect other people spend a lot of time and effort hiding like this as well. Would I be able to overcome my terror of falling apart if I allow myself to rely on others, on you? Or should I be a "cruel optimist" and create hopeful and positive attachments but in awareness that they will not work out in the end?[5] Any option seems too difficult, because the tiniest and most apparently harmless threat of exposure or unreliability that I perceive takes me down in a spiral of terror. Or used to. At some point I was inspired by Chris Kraus and other feminists to embrace anonymous S&M sex. I wanted to experience it as a means to practice vulnerable empowerment, because sadomasochism is a situation in which the dominated exposes and puts herself in the hands of the dominator while being in power through the safe word. I thought this could be an interesting way of experimenting with a sense of vulnerability and being strong, in pain, but at the same time in control. But is this not the same as loving and being open to building together by performing fearless acts of love and by fearlessly accepting love in the terms of the other?

From this place it could be possible to treat vulnerability as a healed scar, a patch of tissue that is still sensitive in certain parts. The scar is nothing other than the atavistic command to become a self-reliant individual who can efficiently manage her own human capital by herself. And what makes that scar heal is not turning inward or isolating ourselves, but opening outward, reaching out to others. Capitalism has prompted us to dream of an ideal individual who can be or is in control of everything. But none of us can be in control. Because we only do exist being-with. And because if we could learn to trust others to make decisions on how to get organized based on what is needed, on what we want, as opposed to organization as a clash of interests and the need to unwillingly compromise, as in democracy, while I secretly both distrust and express disagreement with others. Trusting others through consensus means to give oneself to the other to reach an agreement on what it is best for everyone.

I've come to try to understand my passion for diving as a drive for intimacy. As I linger, fish suddenly stop seeing me as an intruder and embrace me into their world. Perhaps what I love in diving is that feeling of intimacy. Maybe it helps me fill up my own void? My love for riding horses has also something to do with embracing my vulnerability. In teaming up with a horse, we both put our safety in each other's hands, finding balance in agency and trusting oneself to the bodily movements of the other. Motherhood was another solution I also came up with to fill up my own void. This is why I identify with these words Leanne Betamosake Simpson wrote about motherhood and healing:

> when gezhizhawzh needed to heal, and renew herself, she had learned to mother. the stability and rhythm of a new life filled her up. the constant physical contact. the love. the birth ceremony was renewal in itself. no wonder men had to work to not become lost.[6]

So I have established that vulnerability is not a wound but the scar of individualism and thus a kind of kryptonite for all humans. One problem I see if we embrace this is that in our contemporary world, being seen and being exposed overlap with self-marketing. The other side of individualism are the epidemics of indifference and the empathy crisis all of humanity is going through, which are simultaneous to explosions of self-exhibitionism in the public sphere. For instance, Lena Dunham's or Michaela Coel's experiments with narcissistic self-exposure describe how a whole generation perceives itself (and others); or the lethality of terrorist self-exposure, as the voices of victims from all over the planet resonate in the sensible field demanding that we listen to their tragedies; or the ephemeral horror caused by the news in December 2018 exposing the fact that, in Guadalajara, two refrigerator trucks circulated around the state carrying three hundred bodies because there was no place for them at the morgue. Egos without "I's," desubjectified bodies radiating indifference. Many would think it is crazy but I dare to speculate that fragmentation and vulnerability are also tied to our history of colonization. Carlos Rangel, the Venezuelan writer, posits colonial alienation as grounded in uprooting, lack of ties to the earth, the collective sense of not feeling a part of a whole and committed to a communal destiny. According to Rangel, such alienation and detachment lead to non-solidaristic behaviors and generalized selfishness. The higher up a person is in the social and cultural scale, argues Rangel, the more pronounced

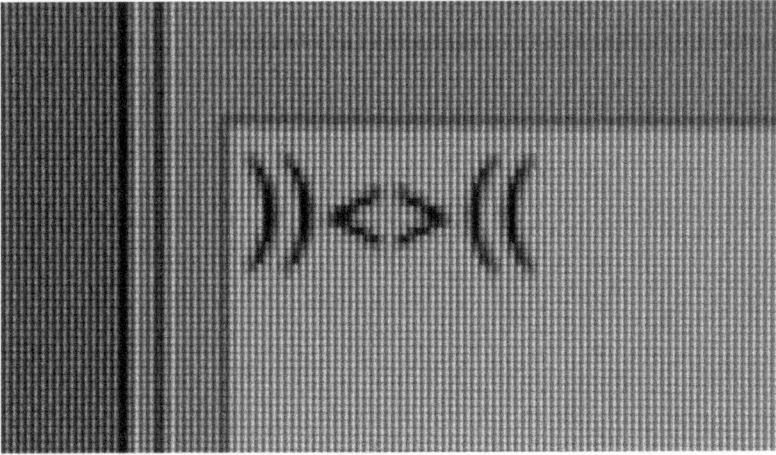

FIGURE 7. "Poop back and forth forever," screenshot from Miranda July's *Me, You and Everyone We Know* (2005), courtesy of the artist.

these feelings will be.[7] Finally, vulnerability is an acknowledgment of the desire for intimacy. So after a long, difficult road, I have come to learn to lie on her like land lies in water. Shadowed green in between, shallows at the edges. A line of seaweed, where the land leans down to lift—or tug— the sea from under.[8]

More about Empathy

According to Franco Berardi, the current lack of possible forms of political organization on the horizon is due to the crisis of empathy lived today by global society.[1] This crisis is rooted first in an anthropological mutation tied to the incorporation of women into the productive labor forces. In many cases, their children were exposed to television or digital screens in such a way that they learned to communicate not through human voice and physical contact, but by means of a screen emitting pre-codified linguistic signals. According to his theory, humans who learned to communicate through technological devices mutated cognitively and are able to connect with others through ready-made codes, but have difficulties *conjugating with* others. That is, some of us are unable to feel others' presence and share a material sensorium that could enable us to feel compassion and empathy toward them. A second reason for the crisis of empathy is due to the conditions of hypercompetition in the work market, which make us see our peers as threats to the means of making a living (or earning prestige, visibility, attention). A social field has been thus generated in which Darwinism has become the main mediator of human relationships. Both situations led to our perception of the other as either consumable and disposable merchandise or as an absolute threat. To that we can add the general desensitization to the problems of others—those whom I barely know as I am absorbed by my own difficulties—and the disappearance of charity as a predominant value in our societies. I am thinking about Luis Buñuel's films *Viridiana* (1961) and *Los Olvidados* (1950), which radically brought into question the morals behind Christian charity, translated to the hypocritical palliative actions and policies known as "social (corporate) responsibility." By this I mean that the traps of religious charity based on "giving what I don't need" have been translated to forms of corporate responsibility that imply "giving to others what I think they need to cover up the mess I am leaving behind making money." To corporate responsibility we can add the neoliberal privatization of collective problems as well as the moral responsibility to *visibilize* the ordeals of others as a prevailing form of politicized aesthetics within the culture industry.

The radical alienation of everyone from everyone else is undoubtedly linked with this excess of audiovisual, artistic, and literary production that shows "the pain of others." For Susan Sontag, to contemplate at a distance the suffering of others facilitated by audiovisual reproduction defines the experience of modernity, and for political theorist Anita Chari. this form of spectatorship is the ultimate form of capitalist alienation.[2]

As for me, I'd like to contribute to this discussion with another piece of the puzzle of the becomings of empathy in our globalized world under the yoke of absolutist capitalism: it has been distorted into a form of despotic empathy that some call "codependence." Codependence is a pathology originating in childhood that manifested in adults who worry too much about the problems of others, who look after someone else as a means to exercise control or who tend to make unnecessary sacrifices for the well-being of others with the unconscious objective of satisfying their own emotional needs. It can be summarized as a form of painful dependency to find approval, meaning, and self-worth. The problem with codependency is that the one a person is codependent to might not be trustworthy because he or she may be undergoing alcohol or drug abuse problems or other self-destructive compulsive behaviors, thereby perpetuating cycles of physical and emotional pain.

The ways collateral damage caused by addiction—or the epidemics of self-destruction haunting the global population—expresses itself are through problems in relationships, behavioral disorders, abuse, and post-traumatic stress syndrome. Relational dysfunctions are strategies that the codependent person created in childhood to survive that get rooted in unhealthy emotional patterns like compulsively looking after someone else or placing oneself in the position of martyr or scapegoat to control or to try to please others at the cost of the self. These behaviors mirror emotional pain trapped in bodies and engraved in our neuronal networks: it is both physical and emotional pain. To be able to survive, a codependent needs to focus on a single person whose emotional instability disconnects her from herself and the things that truly matter. The road to recovery from codependency begins with forgiving oneself for the situations that were beyond her control in childhood, accepting self-hatred and the dark narcissism that had trapped her inside a tragic loop. Codependency (not all psychologists agree that this is the ideal term to define that pathology in behavior) is moreover a kind of distorted, sick empathy generated by fear and pain that causes self-destructive behaviors, which in truth are survival and defense mechanisms.

Empathy, addiction, and codependence are key themes in the work of Leslie Jamison; her first novel, *The Gin Closet* (2010), tells the story of Stella and her alcoholic, overweight aunt Tilly, who was abandoned by her family to live by herself in the Nevada desert. Driven by deep pity, Stella goes to the desert to look for her aunt to give her the news that her grandmother (Tilly's mother) has passed away. Stella finds Tilly submerged in gin, chaos, and poverty and convinces her to move with her to San Francisco with Tilly's son Abe. Stella abandons her mediocre life in New York to live with her aunt and cousin in San Francisco to try to rescue Tilly from her alcoholism. Stella's efforts to rebuild herself looking after her addicted aunt, but from the site of her own darkness (her own addiction, trauma, and anorexia), reveal forms of love and responsibility that tie her (and everyone) to someone else through dysfunction and codependency. Jamison's book ends positing codependency idealistically, as Stella and Abe "rescue" Tilly, convincing her to recover her from addiction. *The Empathy Exams* (2014), the book that Jamison published after *The Gin Closet*, registers instances in which the author places herself in specific places to directly contemplate the pain of someone else: through correspondence and visits to a person sentenced to death row in a US prison; meeting patients with an illness that has not been recognized by medicine and who get together to discuss their symptoms; visiting places in the "third world" plagued by violence (Tijuana, Nicaragua); working as an actor pretending to be in pain to train med students. Interwoven with descriptions of her experiences before the pain of others, Jamison registers her own wounds: a broken heart that also suffers from tachycardia; a broken jaw from falling off a tree in Costa Rica; a trip to Bolivia in which her boyfriend dumps her, a botfly lays eggs under the skin of her ankle, and she grows a maggot; when she is robbed and beaten in Nicaragua. The question that traverses this collection of essays by Jamison is, What do we want to say when we say we feel someone else's pain? She concludes that empathy is a form of compenetration with the suffering of another, akin to traversing a passage or arriving at a new place whose laws we are unaware of. For her, empathy is to choose to pay attention, to expand ourselves by engaging with someone, surpassing ourselves as individuals. This definition of empathy sounds very much like codependency. Her 2018 book, *The Recovering*, is a coming to terms with her own addiction and codependency. With this book, Jamison completes a brilliant trilogy about self-destruction originated in emotional and physical pain that perpetuates patterns of dependency and despotic empathy hindering solidarity, interdependence, and concrete organization with others.

In the past, solidarity ties were administered by religion (through charity) and by the welfare state (social security)—I would not put corporate social responsibility in this category. But not much remains of them except aberrant forms of compassion such as for abandoned or stray dogs and insensibility toward the homeless, people living in misery or precarious situations, global warming refugees or migrants, victims undergoing all kinds of violence.

The irony of generalized indifference coexisting with massive solidarity after the September 19, 2017, earthquake in Mexico is fascinating and symptomatic of something I'm trying to put a finger on. After the 7.1 magnitude earthquake shook the city, thousands of the city inhabitants went out to help clean up the rubble of two middle-class neighborhoods in Mexico City. Citizen solidarity is dangerous for power because as soon as the government was able to react to the tragedy, citizens were pushed away and replaced by the army in the rescue works. Eager to help, citizens moved on to buy basics and groceries for the affected, bringing the goods to dozens of collection centers that sprang up throughout the city. The centers I had the chance to visit were overflowing with food, used clothing, and personal hygiene items. In all of the collection centers, hundreds of volunteers quantified the donations, ordering them in boxes destined for affected families. Thousands of sandwiches were being made to feed the volunteers. There were also donations of equipment to unearth the bodies and clean up the rubble. For more or less three weeks, people mobilized to offer their energies and resources to the cause without ulterior interest (at the most, posting images of their altruism on social media). What is the relationship between such an explosion of compassion and empathy and the indifference that normally prevails amongst the citizens? We must mention that the 1985 earthquake also generated a lot of solidarity and a massive mobilization. This event is even remembered as being the origin of Mexico's Civil Society and had written the script for the 2017 earthquake solidarity: people somehow automatically knew what to do to help. An important issue to consider is that in 2017 help was mainly focused on the most affluent neighborhoods. It is known that homes in working-class neighborhoods and dozens of public schools throughout the city and in the countryside, mainly in Morelos, Puebla, Mexico State, Guerrero, Oaxaca, Veracruz, Tlaxcala, Michoacán, and Hidalgo, suffered structural damage and have not been repaired. Some help was geared to affected rural areas; although abundant and well-meant, it was not always appropriate: dozens of trucks destined to bring help to rural areas were loaded with diapers, razors, deodorants, sanitary pads, bottled water, pasta, and toothbrushes. These things pollute rather than help people on the countryside, as they are not basic needs for people living in rural areas, who most of the time do without them because they can't afford them. After a month of intense help and projects to rebuild houses with PET plastic (transformed into "ecobricks"), the affected who were not helped right away fell into oblivion. Something that I found very troubling with this massive yet partial and misguided demonstration of solidarity was that we have normalized consumption to such an extent that none thought of demanding corporations donate merchandise, considering that their sales had augmented exponentially with the disaster.

The narrative of Michael Haneke's *Happy End* (2017) displays an interweaving of private or individual, communal or familial emotional pain linked to social and capitalist violence, a logic that I'm trying to get at here. The film tells the story of a prominent family who has owned a construction business for at least two generations. The patriarch (Georges Laurent) let his daughter succeed him as president of the company when his wife became terminally ill, and now he spends his days miserable and alone in a wheelchair. Half way through the film, we learn that he tried to kill himself by crashing his car onto a tree; later on, we see him trying to convince an immigrant youth to help him die. He finds an accomplice in one of his granddaughters, Eve (Fantine Harduin), a thirteen–year-old estranged from the family because her father abandoned her and her mother and built a new life without them. Her mother suffered from a mental breakdown and killed herself, so Eve moves in with her father's family in the patriarch's property in Calais. Anne Laurent (Isabelle Huppert) is too busy dealing with the company and with her magnate boyfriend (Toby Jones) to be able to successfully prepare her son Thomas Laurent (Matthiew Kasovitz) to succeed her in the company as CEO. The film begins with an accident at the construction site, and Thomas is responsible for dealing with the ensuing lawsuit. Thomas decides to go see the family of the deceased worker to offer a sum in restitution, but he ends up being beaten up and the problem gets solved by Anne's lawyer on her terms and to the company's favor. Thomas becomes the vessel carrying the family's and social pain around him. He is an alcoholic and in an extraordinary scene, we see him at a Karaoke bar before a meager public singing and dancing to Sia's "Chandelier," a song about getting drunk "'til losing count." In this surprising scene, Thomas's body language echoes the desperation in his voice when he sings "Just holding on for the night," frantically bouncing around the stage, collapsing, and then barely being able to move, he is in so much pain. In the last sequence

of the movie, his mother Anne and her boyfriend have a lunch to celebrate
their engagement with many guests. Thomas shows up to the lunch with a
group of migrants from the Calais jungle (the camp was wiped out that year
by the French police), creating an unbearable clash between the privileged
and the redundant populations who live in absolutely different worlds but
who are interdependent (the privileges of one group of people depend on
the dispossession of the others). The film ends when Eve, after agreeing to
help her grandfather Georges take his own life, records his last moments
with her cellphone right before the rest of the family realize what is going on,
leave the party, and rush to rescue miserable Georges. Alienation, uprootedness, and social and family violence, but also colonial violence, are all
themes addressed by the movie, but especially how they are all interrelated.

What is the relationship between the unprecedented level of disinter-
ested help in aid of earthquake victims and Anita Chari's theory of alienation caused by the excess of images of the pain of others? When I think of
the amount of media—documentaries, news, images, and audiovisual and
literary works—that deals with the emergency situation that the majority
of the population is surviving in, I think about the baroque sculptures
of Christ with torn skin and ulcers all over his body, bleeding slowly to
death. Christ's suffering represented in these sculptures had the purpose
of reminding Christians of the sacrifice the Son of God made in the name
of humanity. We could speculate that the existence of thousands of images
and documents about the "damned of the earth," which we consume and
help proliferate, have the place in our social unconscious that the Catholic Church had given to this representation of the suffering Christ. Perhaps unconsciously we attribute the role of redeemers to those sacrificing
themselves in the name of the well-being of privileged populations. To
the already ubiquitous indifference about the suffering of others, we can
add the criminalization of solidarity at the Mexican-US border and direct
attacks on behalf of Donald Trump's government against groups providing
humanitarian help. For instance, Arizona State University professor Scott
Warren, also a member of the organization "No More Deaths," was put on
trial for offering water and food to two undocumented migrants. Warren
faced three criminal charges for having offered water, food, clean clothes,
and a bed to sleep on to the immigrants in a camp in Ajo, Arizona. In 2019
he was acquitted, but if he had been declared guilty, he could have gotten
a sentence of up to twenty years in jail.

The criminalization of solidarity comes at a moment in which we live and
share distorted and sick forms of empathy, generated by the fear and pain
caused by destructive behavior. As we have seen, though, these ill forms of

caring for others are survival mechanisms established in childhood. And because we share the air we breathe, we are also vulnerable together to natural disasters and global warming. Together also, we share the possibility of healing unhealthy and codependent relationship patterns, forgiving, letting go, recognizing, re-establishing healthy ties of subsistence and interdependence. To acknowledge interdependence between human and nonhuman existence on the planet is vital to our survival, as is expanding ourselves toward something that exceeds us as individuals.

Decolonization

Romantic love is to heteropatriarchy what nationalism is to the State.

Tweet by Yásnaya Elena A. Gil[1]

The affirmation of democracy requires the denial of colonialism, but denying it does not make it go away.

Roxanne Dunbar-Ortiz[2]

From a decolonial standpoint, the Western imperial project is constitutive of modernity and both must be necessarily thought together. How to think of Eros and politics from this standpoint, if intersubjective asymmetrical power relations—mediated by Enlightenment values now being rendered obsolete by absolute capitalism—are the basis of Western societies? Over and over again this quote by Leanne Betamosake Simpson comes to my mind:

> The kind of love that I was interested in, that my characters long for intuitively, is the only kind of love that could liberate them from that horrible legacy of colonial violence. I am speaking about decolonial love ... is it possible to love one's broken-by-the-coloniality-of-power-self in another broken-by-the-coloniality-of-power-person?[3]

What Leanne is saying here intimidates me tremendously. How is love possible after having been broken by colonial relations, which implies relations amongst subjectivities structured by violence, living generation after generation with PTSD? Obviously I have no answer or even real access to this question. Am I even allowed to ask these questions: Can the power-self be forgiven and love a broken-self and be loved back? And, What does one do with the brokenness between?

While I am aware that decolonization is key in current struggles because anticapitalism is not enough to address all of the planet's problems, Eros in conjunction with politics seems to provide a provisional answer in terms of the political challenges "we" are facing in today's extractivist (still colonial) landscape. And yet, when discussing decolonization within the context of "Eros and Politics," I could imagine Leanne's impatience with someone like me bringing this up. Perhaps the starting question needs to be, How can people begin to recognize, accept, respect, and break through the barrier of prejudice brought about by centuries of oppression, rejection, domination, and colonization? I feel that we need to look toward the root of the problem beyond being able to recognize colonized people's oppression and our (descendants of colonizers) role in that oppression. To turn the mirror toward ourselves and find the deeper logic at work in colonial brokenness, which is tied not only to all the discourses and practices that enable and hide intersubjective asymmetrical power relations but also to Modernity's logic of domination and extraction, not from a decolonizing perspective, but starting from the fact that we are settlers. In our neoliberal era, subjectivities are being further shattered by absolute capitalism and its crisis of human, environmental, and interpersonal relations manifested, for instance, through femicide or in the transformation of the mechanisms of love (feelings, emotions, seduction, desire) into commodities. Brokenness also stems or is shattered further by capitalist "productivity," which means dispossessing peoples not only of their territories, but also their labor, bodies, language, lives. These forms of violence have been justified by the production of the abundance of goods so that a portion of the global population can have anything we want, so we can live "good" lives designed by technocracy, adorned by culture and design, so we no longer have to make a living with the sweat of our brows, and that originary populations and mestizos— Indigenous peoples "de-Indigenized" by the State, as Yásnaya Elena A. Gil puts it, are cheap labor, cannon fodder, and folklore to the Nation-State.[4] As the communist idea of cooperation is obsolete, excess production and labor achieved through violence and dispossession provide the general feeling that we can have comfort while being relieved of the pressure of contributing to society and of the feeling that we are needed by others.

The sense of relief felt by not needing or being needed by others to fulfill our needs is what leads Theodor Twombly to a love affair with Samantha, an AI dispositive. In Spike Jonze's 2013 film *Her*, the ideal is a painless, disembodied love relationship grounded on abhorrence of interdependency and attachment. Maggie Nelson formulates this generalized feeling/tendency/ condition of contemporary existence in this manner: "The Self without sympathetic attachments is either a fiction or a lunatic. . . . [Yet] dependence is scorned even in intimate relationships, as though dependence were incompatible with self-reliance rather than the only thing that makes it possible."[5] Disembodied detachment from others comes with self-reliance through technology; in that way, *Her* is not only a dystopian sci-fi exacerbation of some tendencies from the present, but reflects disembodied detachment hypostatizing, as, for instance, in Amazon Go, completely automated convenience stores with no cashers and total monitoring with facial recognition and smartphones to buy merchandise. The condition of possibility of both *Her* and Amazon Go is based on a relationship between self and others premised on disembodied detachment and lives devoid of meaning grounded on a fundamental act of violence: the destruction of the lives of others (i.e., Congolese people for coltan, the mineral used to make Smartphones and computers). While *Her* fulfills first-wave feminism's (and Silicon Valley's) dream of women becoming rational consciousness by doing away with the biological body—like men were enabled to transcend by rational thought, as Simone de Beauvoir explains—Amazon Go materializes capitalism's dream to make (human) labor disappear. There is even now the tendency to make affective labor physically disappear, for instance with Care.Coach, the startup that offers elderly care through screens operated by staff in a remote location manifesting as avatars interacting with the customers through screens. Nowadays, human contact in the realms of learning, living, and dying has become a luxury good, especially after the COVID-19 pandemic.[6]

In November 2017, the destructive principle behind disembodied detachment expressed itself as the demise of tolerance at the UN Climate Summit in Bonn, when California governor Jerry Brown told Indigenous protesters demanding an end to fracking on their lands, "Let's put *you* in the ground."[7] This event points at the fact that the absolute obliteration of difference is not only the condition of possibility of capitalist expansion, but somehow, the ideal condition of modern man, and that violence is actually the permanent mediator between the self and the body, the self and others, humans and nature, and among culturally differentiated human communities.

The current situation of Indigenous peoples in Canada gives me hope, as I feel that it stands out from the rest of the world because of their recent and ongoing upheaval with mobilizations like "Idle No More." There is also the unprecedented Truth and Reconciliation Report, in which the government of Canada acknowledged the wrongs that were done to First Nations, Inuit, and Métis peoples, who had been forced to live in residential schools, stolen away from their parents and communities, violently severed from their cultural roots.

When it comes to State recognition of the damage against originary populations throughout five centuries, we are not only far behind Canada, but in sheer denial. Yásnaya Elena A. Gil, a young *ajuuk* or *mije* writer from San Pedro and San Pablo Ayutla, Oaxaca, has warned us against the "shadows" inherent to the solidarity of non-Indigenous peoples who get involved or who are interested in vindicating Indigenous rights. While she recognizes that there are valuable contributions by non-Indigenous persons to their struggle, she argues others get involved superficially, only in discourse, relating to Indigenous people only as prefabricated images of alterity celebrating folklore, or by appropriating their rituals and ancestral medicinal methods without really knowing them, thereby preserving the myth of the good savage.[8] These means of idealizing originary peoples perpetuate subtle and not so subtle forms of discrimination. In this context, Indigenous voices have only begun to transcend their status as white noise and as poetry in danger of extinction to being voices taken seriously in a Mexican State that recognizes itself as plurinational but from the standpoint of the superficial varnish of culture. In the meantime, the State continues systematic genocide, dispossession, and other forms of oppression with the complicit silence of its criollo and mestizo citizens against Indigenous peoples. Comparable to Canada's residential schools is the experiment inaugurated by Plutarco Elías Calles in 1925, La Casa del Estudiante Indígena (The Home of the Indigenous Student) in Mexico City, where a group of "pure Indians" were interned. Once "civilized," they were meant to return to their communities as "culturalizing agents" and integrate them to the monolingual homogenous Nation-State. It seems that the interned were kidnapped and living in terrible conditions, and so many of them either died or escaped.[9] But even if the Mexican State would apologize for these experiments, recognizing the five-hundred-year-old damage against originary populations, instituting a legal apparatus for restitution, what good would it do and for whom? What would restitution look like? Would that imply that non-Indigenous Mexicans would recognize the legacy of historical and remaining colonial structures? I am thinking of a similar gap between legislation and society that exists regarding the achievements of the LGBTQIA movement in Mexico: So much has been achieved in terms of rights and recognition in the past ten years (including rights to marriage and adoption), and yet we live in a homophobic society that discriminates against married homosexual couples and that lobbies against homoparental families. For instance, my daughter attends a school that can be held legally liable if not showing tolerance

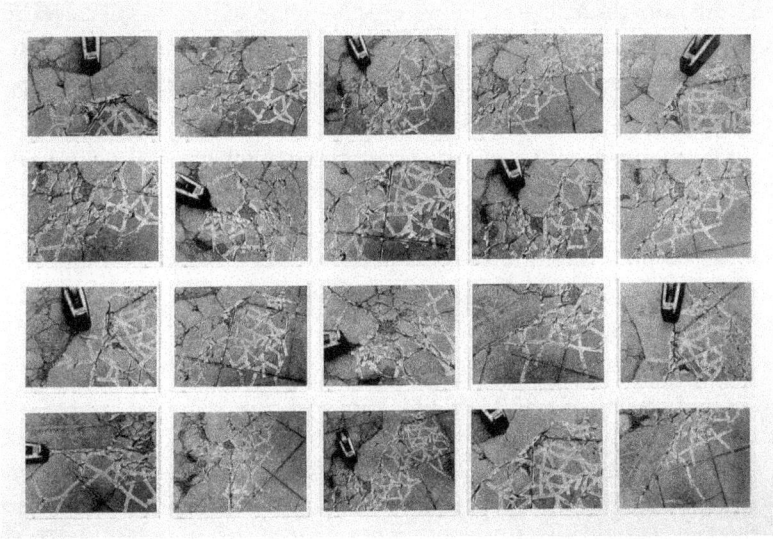

FIGURE 8. Silvia Gruner, Reparar (1999; Repairing), © Silvia Gruner, 1999, courtesy of the artist.

to homoparental families, but there are homophobic families, and LGBT+ and gender issues in general are lacking in the school's curriculum. In the 2018 presidential election, independent candidate Margarita Zavala concurred with a strategic pro-family right-wing position. If not through the legal apparatus, where and how are these battles to be fought? Let's recall that the feminist movement achieved huge ground by lobbying to legislate for equal and reproductive rights for women. In the case of Indigenous peoples and decolonization, how do we ground the discussion back into society beyond obvious racism and inequality, but make it make sense in everyday life? The same goes for decolonization. Unfortunately, ours is still a colonial Nation and we have been pushed back decades in thought and discussions around this issue by the current Mexican president, Andrés Manuel López Obrador. Right after he came to power (following similar gestures by Bolivian president Evo Morales or Venezuela's Nicolás Maduro), he demanded on behalf of Indigenous Mexicans that Philip IV (as representative of the Spanish monarchy) and the Pope (representing the Catholic Church), apologize and demand forgiveness from Indigenous peoples whose rights (what is known today as "human rights") have been violated since 1521. The demand for historical reconciliation is premised on the logic that the colonial project ended with the declaration of Mexican Independence, as if the Spanish and their descendants disappeared by declaring themselves to be "Mexicans."[10] But even if we cannot unbecome settlers by getting the fuck out from the land—as I know some Jewish Israelis are—will it ever be possible to inhabit together (colonizers and colonized) on incommensurable terms, different than those imposed by the legitimization of occupation represented by the Nation-State?

At a global scale, there are two political standpoints of Indigenous and marginalized peoples in relationship to their struggle against the Nation-State: the nationalist and the anti-imperialist standpoint. Anti-imperialism implies adopting a critical stand toward the tools, concepts, vocabularies, and organization practices that characterize contemporary landscapes of struggle. That is to say, the point of departure of anti-imperialist struggle is the fact that the tools we use to change unjust structures stem precisely from those structures. This also implies recognizing that the model of the Nation-State is bourgeois and white, and that it will never guarantee justice for everyone. Part of the problem is to recognize that we will have Nation-States for a long while, and part of contemporary activism is teaching and motivating people to imagine something different from that institution. For its part, the nationalist standpoint understands the State as a *pharmakon* (poison and medicine), that civil society without the structure of the Nation-State is lacking a civil contract that would guarantee civil society its rights, and that it would be problematic to rely on NGOs because they tend to be led by self-proclaimed entrepreneurs subsidized by corporate interests. That is why the nationalist standpoint vouches not for dismantling the Nation-State but for protecting citizenship, and although the State is the administrator of global capital, believes the State is not "bad" but a tool to guarantee rights.[11] In that sense, we could evoke the Zapatista, who practice autonomy while recognizing that they are symbolically part of the Mexican nation and territory. Yásnaya's stand is that the construction of a nation needs to acknowledge the existence of the many nations that compose it, each with its own history and language as well as particular identities and forms of life. Part of the ongoing problem is that the Mexican State apparatus, the Mexican judicial system, for instance, are far from being inclusive. Yásnaya writes how Mexican courts lack translators, hindering originary populations' access to justice; there are many unjustly incarcerated Indigenous persons because of lack of translators. Or how bureaucrats working in State institutions in Indigenous territories do not know the languages, or that information in hospitals or about social programs is only in Spanish although addressed to them. This helps perpetuate racism and injustice, normalizing and incubating repressive pedagogies implanted on Indigenous bodies who are made to believe that their languages "do not count." The State, moreover, follows the mandate of modernization by repressing and expelling "the Indians" from themselves. As a political apparatus, moreover, democracy implies erasing the colonial past that remains silenced. This past is taboo too in academia, where originary peoples exist either as subjects of knowledge or as idealized communal entities of utopian alternative community organization. If for Indigenous feminists, as Silvia Rivera Cusicanqui argues, patriarchy and colonialism are the same thing because women are "sacrifice zones," and devastation of the commons and sexual violence are part of the spoliation, conquest and colonial dispossession machinery,[12] is it our goal to decolonize Modernity? Could that be possible?

In a letter addressed to Zapatista women, Sylvia Marcos quotes a paragraph from their 2018 declaration: "And that other thing, very other and very hard, is being indigenous Zapatista woman. So we tell you, sister and comrade, that we are not asking you to come fight for us, because we are also not going to fight for you. Each knows their road, their means, their times, their world."[13] Here, Zapatista women demand the recognition of the intersectionality of women's struggle, that we not idealize or try to "save" them. Sylvia Marcos answers that we, feminists from "outside," are not conscious of the fact that we bear within us the "capitalist neoliberal frame as well as the racist and classist structure that frames and dominates us." She calls it "interior epistemic racism," an unconscious enemy that perpetuates racism and dispossession and that operates by invisibilizing the colonial matrix of multiple dispossession that traverses the bodies of Indigenous women. Without a doubt, it is our task to become conscious of interior epistemic racism from the standpoint of intersectionality, and we should also be attentive to the incipient Indigenous voices in public space that celebrates diversity blindly. As an example, I can think of the disgusting condescension inherent to the preface to Yásnaya's recently published essay collection by Federico Navarrete, the most highly respected voice in Mexican Academia on racism. Throughout his text, Navarrete repeats many times the adjective "freshness" or "refreshing" to describe Yásnaya's writing. He admires her fluency in Castilian as well in the languages of digital platforms. He praises her for writing an "intimate and sincere diary," for her "intellectual honesty" and "sincere modesty" and because her text is a sign of the "flourishing and renaissance of contemporary Indigenous thought" in Mexico. Navarrete moreover, praises Yásnaya's lecture at the Colegio Nacional in 2019, which she delivered in her mother tongue, *ayuuk* or *mije*, the first one of its kind in that prestigious institution in Mexico. Yásnaya's declaration on linguistic diversity was celebrated while I should note that the Colegio Nacional is made up of a body of eighty-eight members, half of whom are dead, and 90 percent of whom are white men, amongst them male literary dinosaurs.

Among the members of the Colegio Nacional are no women or Indigenous writers, although one of its members is astronomer Guillermo Haro. Haro is Elena Poniatowska's ex-husband, who told her (not a member of the Colegio Nacional although one of the most respected writers alive today in Mexico) whenever he saw her writing, that she was wasting time with her "pendejaditas." Navarrete's preface to Yásnaya's book and the invitation from the Colegio Nacional, a misogynist and racist institution that simulates democracy by inviting Yásnaya to speak, are signs of current epistemic racism in Mexico, where self-complacent beings, content with sharing space with writers like Yásnaya in the national cultural panorama, are unaware of debates on decolonization and appropriation and of the enormous task we, as criollos and mestizos, have before us in terms of decolonization.

From the point of view of Eve Tuck and Wayne Yang's text "Decolonization as Metaphor," decolonization may easily fall prey to becoming a mere discourse in education, scholarship, and cultural production, turning decolonization into a metaphor, further retrenching settler colonialism, which implies rationalizing and maintaining unfair social structures.[14] For Tuck and Yang, decolonization is something other than civil and human rights-based social justice processes, and it needs to be premised, first and foremost, on the recognition that settlers have been using Indigenous land (and bodies) for centuries as a source for capital. Therefore, the current absolute capitalist appetite for "natural resources" means that the colonial processes of extraction and dispossession are ongoing. Decolonization thus requires an un*settling* restructuring beyond the logic of extraction and dispossession that needs to be grounded on epistemological, ontological, and cosmological relationships.

Bearing this in mind, there is so much work that needs to get done, and so I feel I am not completely ready to disavow the Eros/politics conjuncture. For Alain Badiou, they are opposites, as love begins where politics ends. By this he means that politics constitutes a truth procedure centered on the collective. The truth procedure will reveal whether the collective can embrace equality (or difference), integrate what is heterogeneous. He therefore defines politics as a measurement of the capacity of individuals to organize and make decisions collectively.[15] In turn, he posits love as about people being able to handle difference, and to experience the world from the point of view of difference. But for Badiou, love and politics need to be kept separate. The Christian "to love one another" remains in the realm of ethics, as a quest for truth about difference which must be rigorously separated from politics. But perhaps grounding politics in trust in difference rather than being suspicious of it (like reactionaries and fascists are always suspicious of difference in the name of identity) might lead us somewhere, while acknowledging that equality—in the sense of an "exact equal" (as the French expect French Arabs to become within their model of integrationism, as opposed to the Anglo-Saxon model of multiculturalism)—is a myth. From a radical Western point of view, equality should be substituted by radical, fluid, and open difference. But from a decolonial point of view, radical difference is not enough. Tuck and Yang demand to seek opportunities of solidarity within the incommensurable, as opposed to what is different or common. Recognizing what is incommensurable means, for example, acknowledging that while Europeans and descendants of Europeans in North America and in the "Global South" may not be on the receiving end of oppressive relations, colonial violence in fact impacts *everyone* and that privilege is hierarchical and racialized.[16] Tuck and Yang ask us to understand that decolonization is not about reversing positions of dominance, but repatriating land, abolishing slavery, and dismantling empire.

Decolonizing requires a change in order of the world. From Tuck and Yang's point of view, there is too much that is incommensurable (relationship to land, histories, memories). And so the question of love and politics in our (inevitably Western) terms and its relevance in accounting for an ethics of incommensurability kept haunting us. I have many reasons why I am convinced that we need not only to gain awareness of our status as settlers and, from that standpoint, adopt other values that are nonmodern—basically become aware that the whole of capitalist Western society is predatorial and think how we could overcome that— and that would enable living together in incommensurability as opposed to further disembodiment, detachment, and destruction. I have in mind here Leanne Simpson's notion of "resurgence," which implies (put in Western terms) a map out of colonial thinking by confirming Indigenous lifeways or alternative ways of being in the world: a form of renaissance that is simultaneously resistance.[17] Where and how can bridges be built? How to acknowledge the incommensurability of brokenness when we (you and I), too, are broken?

I feel there is so much despair everywhere at the moment. Right now, I think to love means to resist the obscenity of the market and the current political hegemonic denigration of difference. But there is also so much to learn and do.

FIGURE 9. Robert Venturi, *Las Vegas Style*, Las Vegas (1966), courtesy of Venturi, Scott Brown and Associates, Inc.

FIGURE 10. Denise Scott Brown, *Robert Venturi à la Magritte*, Las Vegas (1966), courtesy of Venturi, Scott Brown and Associates, Inc.

Maternity Slavery Rebellion Creativity Jouissance

An article from the *Guardian* reports that an "expert in happiness" discovered that unmarried and childless women are happier than married mothers and that, while a married man is healthier and will live longer than a woman, the risks of physical and mental illness increase for a woman with marriage and children.[1] Leaving aside the problem that "happiness experts" now diagnose and evaluate society, the information revealed by the article illuminates a problem of social organization at its basis: the conditions of inequality that women are still living posited—in neoliberal terms—as "unhappiness" indexes, which is obviously and obliviously the opposite of "the personal is the political."

One of the battles feminist women of the second wave fought half a century ago was to join the work market because they considered that women's oppression had an economic cause and solution: what Silvia Federici and others posited as the "patriarchate of salary." After a long and difficult battle, women achieved access to the public sphere and were able to join the work force. Having taken the reins of their own reproduction, they had placed maternity not as an inescapable obligation, but as one choice amongst other life choices. Our salaries, however, remain considerably inferior to men's, partly because this society calls all women to become mothers. For this reason, we are considered to be less competitive and thus less desirable in the labor market. This is because when we become mothers, we have difficulties in meeting the demands from work: when a kid falls ill, we must miss work, we have to ask permission to leave early when our children have a festival or a party, we need to get home not too late to look after the kids and take care of domestic work, and so on. Ironically, because a working woman who is a mother has more responsibilities than other workers, she would never risk or give up a salary, as meager as it may be. This is why mothers are required to perform certain difficult and demanding tasks in gas stations, agroindustry, sweatshops, public relations, and teaching, working under dire conditions and for terrible pay. And because many families in this country are sustained by women, we have to assume more responsibilities by choice or circumstance but also because of need. Consider F, who got divorced from her alcoholic, unfaithful husband, and then, two years later, the father of her daughter began a process of transition. The kid doesn't know how to handle her father's gender transition and doesn't want to know anything about the person she became (or revealed herself to be). As a way to pressure their daughter to see her, the ex-spouse stopped paying alimony to my friend, who had to take up a second job to take care of the expenses. Or there is P, who became a widow a few days after her son turned one; she was left to her own devices with an old car, two motorbikes, a dog, and two cats (and a baby boy) as inheritance. Her in-laws helped to get the company where her husband worked (he died in a work accident) to assure her son's education throughout university, but she has to take care of the rest of the expenses, living in an extremely precarious situation. Each case is evidence that single mothers solve problems by self-exploiting, producing, and reproducing until our bodies and minds collapse and we need to spend our savings in restorative physical and mental therapies.

From the standpoint of the difficulties of being a single mother, Phyllis Schlafly's defense of family values makes some sense. Phyllis Schlafly led a conservative movement in the 1970s against feminism and abortion and campaigned successfully against the ratification of the Equal Rights Amendment to the US Constitution. Schlafly believed that American women were the most privileged creatures in the world for being enabled by their husbands to devote themselves to their homes and children. She thus led a movement to defend traditional family values, recruiting women who were terrified of being forced out into the job market to compete with men and afraid that the liberals would draft their daughters into the army. Schlafly is portrayed in the FX series *Miss America* (2020), fighting for her cause in talk shows and lecture halls, lobbying with politicians in Washington and across America to promote her "Stop the E.R.A." campaign. In the series, her secret wish to become a real politician and the ways she is always "shrinking" herself before her husband are hinted at. Also we see that her political skills and mailing list are remarkable—it is said that her mailing list helped Ronald Reagan win the 1980 election. Schlafly attended law school and delegated the care of her children and home to her sister-in-law—in a sort of unavowed feminism—and lives with the contradiction of defending family values that keep women trapped doing reproductive labor while desperately wanting to become a real, respected politician and achieve recognition in a world dominated by men. The series ends with a scene in which Schlafly bakes a perfect cake, demonstrating that she is successfully performing the values she fought for and unable to take a step forward and break away from them, which is her secret and deepest desire. Perhaps the figure of Schlafly is a reminder of sorts, to resist the self-exploitation of embracing productive and reproductive labor?

In a way, the price of our independence on the terms of and within heteropatriarchal capitalist society—that is to say, the power we achieved to earn a salary—has been to have to assume the double burden of productive and reproductive work. For reasons that I have been trying to elucidate in the essays in this book, this load is assumed in the context of a crisis of relationality, in which our networks of support tend to be unstable, precarious, or costly monetarily or emotionally. The difficulties of maternity under heteropatriarchy also derive from the fact that reproductive labor is considered to be an uncomfortable remnant of society because it does not provide surplus value directly, but rather absorbs unpaid or badly paid labor and is thus denigrated and invisibilized. In this context, nurturing is relevant only to the capitalist system as a niche of consumption and to groom a future reserve of workers and consumers. That is to say, in spite of denigrating reproductive work, the capitalist system counts on women's exploitation for its continuity. Another aspect we need to consider to understand the difficult conditions under which we exercise our maternity is the cultural requirement—through individualism and the neoliberal obligation of fending for ourselves—to create solid reproductive-care networks: parents, grandparents, extended families, friends, or siblings are now usually busy with personal projects focused on productive work, in constructing a "career." One of the consequences is exercising maternity in deep solitude along with political loneliness, lacking social and political rights that support maternity. This is why many women live maternity as undesirable, a burden, or a sacrifice. Not even the superficial mystique of May 10 (Mother's Day in Mexico) is capable of ameliorating the sensation of living choked with responsibilities, frustration, exhaustion. Sometimes, like Hollywood archetypes, we get drunk or high in gatherings just to feel liberated together during moments we steal from our maternal responsibilities. Can we put aside the yoke of the new "must" that is imposed on women in spite of the achievements of feminist struggles of the twentieth century? Women molded by heteropatriarchal and pharmacological "femininity" are raising their children while bringing a salary home—making barely enough money to pay to delegate care of their children or domestic tasks. This new "must" of motherhood, moreover, comes with the mandate to become "helicopter moms" whose sole priority is to raise their children to make them "successful" from childhood. Helicopter moms are excessively invested in their children's development and activities to the point of being present in their lives obsessively and despotically. This form of exercising maternity is linked to the need for some sort of authenticity or meaning, to validate one's own life and the social order through the figure of "the offspring."

Over a decade ago, queer theorist Lee Edelman published a controversial book in which he describes how extra-political values had begun to infiltrate US policy making, specifically, pro-family, right-wing values and their focus on children's protection linked to opposition to and prohibition of abortion (or Schlafly reloaded). Edelman explains how pro-family values are perfectly in sync with the capitalist system's needs: they imply the inversion of human capital in the medium and long term. Edelman describes how at the end of the 1990s, Bill Clinton began to portray himself as a "concerned and hard-working father devoted to his children," a "daddy bear" and head of a "political home."[2] This is how the offspring became the horizon of politics, the ghost beneficiaries of all political intervention, an order that gives us back the image of the offspring as an image of the future that the political intervention is taking care of. An imaginary was thus created based on the future survival of the political body through procreation.

Edelman takes up P. D. James's novel *The Children of Men* (1992), which describes an infertile planet that might potentially be reborn through the miracle of birth: if there is a baby, there is future and redemption—also one of the premises of the dystopian extreme right-wing world drawn in Margaret Atwood's *The Handmaid's Tale*. In this logic, the meaning of politics, according to Edelman, is based on a reproductive futurism that perpetuates as a reality the fantasy of assuring the survival of the social and the offspring as an imaginary register. Edelman posits a form of queer opposition against this coercive belief in the value of the future grounded on the offspring, a reality in which children function as the basis of a kind of secular theology that shapes our collective narratives and meanings underlying the capitalist machinery. He proposes queer sexuality to oppose this civil order, exercising different forms of love and kinship that put less weight on the assertion of an oppositional political identity and more on opposing a politics of a fantasy that governs to realize, always in an indefinite future, imaginary identities that mark a fetishistic fixation on heteronormativity. What to do before the imminent sacralization of the offspring that keep us women obliged to produce and reproduce ourselves, in complicity with the capitalist regime?

Because, in spite of Edelman and the feminists who struggled against the imposition of maternity, heteronormative social imaginaries based on imagined futures and reproduction are still intact, and "the duty to be a mother" still prevails; once I heard Judith Butler state that every woman who chooses not to be a mother carries certain social stigma. And it is true, they are considered to be dangerous, suspicious, weird, because not only did they refuse to perpetuate our species, but they are also sparing society their maternal suffering. It is clear, however, that not all women are meant to become mothers. I have witnessed imposed maternities and understood how such an imposition can completely destroy a woman and her children. "Being" a mother is a state of being which is not interexchangeable, transferrable, temporal: it means being in charge of another body, to be its supplement so that the child can survive until she can become independent. Bearing in mind that as humans, we have "neoteny," which means that we are the mammal species that takes longest to mature to become independent: dependency for at least eighteen years is not optional. The problem is that in our capitalist societies, raising children comes into conflict with a woman's desires and needs, with the individual principles of freedom and autonomy, with societal and a partner's demands, and clearly with the capitalist demand to be hyperproductive.

If I had to sum it up, I would define maternity as a state of being in which one deals with one's own shit while taking care of the shit of someone else who has no clue how to deal with his or her own shit. My hypothesis is very literally inspired by Mary Kelly's *Post-Partum Document* (1973–1979), a work of art in which the artist registers the development of her son Kelly Barrie from the moment of birth until he is five years old. A collection of dirty baby diapers, among other objects linked to a child's upbringing and development, are meaningful aspects of the piece onto which Kelly has written reflections about her relationship to her son. What I love the most about Kelly's piece is that it shows maternity as a complex and difficult relationship in which both parts adapt and develop in tandem. Not long ago, I was immersed in my thoughts, dealing with my own shit, while driving to the countryside, and suddenly my subject of reproduction, then eight years old, announced that she needed urgently to go to the bathroom because she felt a cramp announcing diarrhea. I panicked because the idea of stopping on the highway made me feel extremely vulnerable and there was nowhere apparently safe to park for a pit stop for many kilometers ahead. I gave her a plastic bag so she could do what she had to do. While driving, I convinced her to use the bag, encouraging her with sweet words. Then I congratulated her and tried to clean up the mess a bit with the napkins that had wrapped our sandwiches. As soon we reached a toll booth, I stopped to clean up the shit. That day, I had to deal with her shit and with my own shit, which ironically had been generated by a conflict with my partner about being a mother.

Now, to the hardships of maternity, we can add that women who are mothers and who do creative work must have not only two but three or four jobs, because creative work is rarely remunerated or is badly paid and this is why we have to have an extra income to sustain ourselves and supplement our creative work. I fully subscribe to the way Lina Meruane posits the challenge that women creators face from this perspective: if, for a childless creator, having two jobs is difficult and comes in the way of creation, for the creator who is a mother, it is even harder to find spaces to devote herself to creation because she shares "the room of her own" with a son or daughter who neither knows limits nor respects doors. That is why, for a woman who creates, as for someone who lives in poverty, the boy or girl can be perceived as a burden, as an internal enemy.[3]

But things can even get more difficult if we are moms who create if we consider that in the culture field, women are still trapped in certain roles as producers, translators, administrators, curators, organizers. That is to say, more than being creators, we are still considered to be "guardians" of culture, as we are expected to maintain the patriarchal cultural contract. This is in addition to having to overcome the condition imposed on women: not to speak our mind, to make ourselves smaller not to occupy too much space or to threaten men, to repress our own hysteria generated by heteropatriarchy, and not to show too much anger.

For all these reasons, it is three times harder for women than it is for men to achieve credibility and have a career in the creative field. The difficulties reside concretely in the fact that under heteropatriarchy, mothers only exist to raise and feed their children. As a creative woman *I am out of my place*. In contrast, the myth of the man who engenders books from the genius of his womb, fed by years of conferences and his own mind, has a life administered by an army of (female) assistants. To me, writing is a true feat: I need to delegate Layla's care to a babysitter or nanny, pay for some extracurricular class (French, aerial dance, gymnastics, swimming), or send her to summer camp. Writing actually *costs* me, and that is why I need an additional salary to cover the extra expenses. Clearly, when women manage to stand out in the creative field it is not because they followed men's example of abandoning their children, but because they counted on help or had the fortune to pay for the care of their children. I remember coming across a text by academic Margo Glanz—or was it Margit Frenk?—thanking the Indigenous women who raised their children for her so she could devote her life to research; there is also a text by Ángeles Mastretta in which she explains that her writing regime was for many years marked by the hours of absence of their children at school, while someone else took care of the house and of dropping them off and picking them up from school. Tragic cases abound of women, with children but lacking the means to devote themselves to writing, either abandoning writing for a while, like Lucia Berlin, or giving up, or killing themselves, like Silvia Plath. The suffering generated by the need to stop "creating" in order to "procreate" fits perfectly into the biological experience of the female body and with the suffering linked to the sacrifice tied to maternity. The suffering that originates in renouncing creativity is analogous to the pain undergone by giving birth: a natural female destiny that gives way to the archetype of female experience as passive suffering.

In a truly terrifying text, somewhat reminiscent of the dark aspects of Mary Kelly's logbook of her son's development, journalist and writer Daniela Rea registers the ambivalent feelings she deals with as a mother and writer. She describes the thousands of interruptions, the anger, frustration, useless discussions, and tantrums, of sitting in front of the computer and having energy only to contemplate the screen, the terror of the sensation of losing herself by devoting her life to maternity:

> I have been becoming, little by little, when I wake up at night so you can squeeze my breast, salt, energy. When I cry because you cry. When I leave the room and I leave you crying because I don't know how to calm you down. Also during nights like this that I was able to put you to sleep in my arms and I'm still alive. [. . .] I hate my life. My body. My mornings. [. . .] All of sudden, I have the sensation that my life is this that I didn't want: disgusted by everything, all the time.[4]

Rea's document is tremendous; her afflictions are analogous to the suffering generated by the condition of oppression, of slavery, of living locked down in a concentration camp. Part of the problem of the suffering originated by the degradation of the lives of women by maternity is that we run the risk of transmitting it to our daughters. It goes without saying that many of us grew up feeling guilt and hatred derived from our own mothers' motherhood experiences. When the system takes away from us our egos, bodies, labor, and we live tired and furious, it becomes more difficult to raise our children. That is why, and in order not to repeat this pattern, we need

to be conscious of the problem and avoid becoming vehicles of the heredi-
tary cycles of feminine frustration and self-negation. It is also key to find
strategies to educate not only in spite of and against heteropatriarchy, but
also against the hedonism of the neoliberal culture that has infiltrated into
the ways we raise our children by neglect, in the sense of pleasing our children either materially or by not setting boundaries for them. Many times it
is easier to give into children's demands for instant gratification and go on
multitasking. We are, however, transmitting to them a distorted idea of love:
a dynamics of punishment and reward. Thus, the mothers of "little mon-
sters" have become mere instruments to satisfy their desires, an approach
that children interpret as acts of love.

If being a mother becomes something extremely difficult for the reasons
I have tried to sketch out above, the site to resist affliction or impotence
generated by maternity would be for me to go beyond accusatory feminism
that makes us lament having reproduced ourselves at the service of heteropatriarchy or capitalism or having fulfilled a social role based on a "natural
destiny." To resist is to transform maternal suffering into something useful
that can take us beyond that experience, to enlighten ourselves and grow
as women; to resist maternal suffering is to rethink it through the place of
the social crisis of relationality, the lack of shared meaning in our societies,
to create stable networks of interdependence and care based on solidarity.
Maternity is made up of bonding, something societies and communities
now lack. To reinvent maternal suffering is not to fall into the temptation
of making demands to the State to "recognize" us or give us perks of social
welfare. To resist is to link creativity and reproduction together, building
a shared site of joyful nurturing and healing and moving toward a future
other world. To set the basis of an antiheteropatriarchal maternity, Adrienne
Rich's investigations can be useful. She reveals that in matriarchal cultures,
the main creative force is female. That is to say, maternity used to be not
only a social function or a natural destiny, but the essence of the potential
of transformation to continue life.[5] Matriarchal societies conceived creative force intrinsically tied to maternity as a necessary transformative force.
Under matriarchy, the link between creation and reproduction resides in
the fact that existence emerges potentially from the female body. From this
perspective, it is probable that the French second-wave feminists were mis-
taken in conceiving *écriture feminine* as symmetrically opposed to masculine
writing. Theoreticians and philosophers like Luce Irigaray, Hélène Cixous,
or Julia Kristeva grounded their concept of female writing in opposition to
the analogy of the phallus and the writer's pen and ejaculation as expression.
For them, feminine writing was also linked to the orgasm, defining writing

FIGURE 11. Drawing by Layla, image courtesy of the author.

as a series of expressive waves that fluctuate in intensity (I wonder if these women ever ejaculated). In our society centered on machinic production, bodily reproduction as a creative act is taboo. That is why, like Adrienne Rich, we need to imagine a world in which every woman is the genius presiding her body to generate new meanings and change the place of reproduction in our societies, in the name of a different future.

Voice Desire Body Difference Love

Marguerite Duras's novella *La Maladie de la mort* is minimalist, which means that it is written in simple language and the narrative is not transparent as to the actions unfolding. It can be described as a nonlineal dialogue that describes sites of pain, frustration, what is present and absent. Its main topic is the impossibility of love parting from a tension established between gender and sexuality. The premise of *La Maladie de la mort* is that a homosexual man hires a heterosexual woman to stay all weekend with him with the purpose that by the end of the week, they may experience love. The premise contains, however, its own failure: love is neither an act of the will or a monetary transaction. In this way, in the proposal a tension is already established between the man's homosexuality and the woman's heterosexuality. The "you" wants to learn to love and his "illness" is due to this wrong premise, because love is, at the start, impossible between them. In the novella, Duras sets forth a devastating version of modern sexuality and gender relations engendered from the abyss established between men and women based on the irrationality of passionate relationships and eroticism: "You cannot recognize the penetration of bodies, you can never acknowledge it. You will never be able to. When you cried, it was only for yourself and not by the admirable impossibility of reaching it through the difference that separates us."[1]

The notion of eroticism drawn here by Duras is reminiscent of Georges Bataille's:

We are discontinuous beings, individuals who die isolated in an unintelligible adventure; but what remains with us is nostalgia of lost continuity. It is not difficult to bear the situation that leaves us grounded on individuality borne out of chance, in the perishable individuality that we are. While we have an anguished desire to last forever and that is perishable, we are obsessed with the first continuity, that which ties us to being in a general mode.[2]

For Bataille as for Duras, beings long for recovering that originary lost continuity, but it is impossible to achieve it either through desire and non-desire. That is the malady of death. Filmmaker Cathérine Berillat translated Duras's text to the script for her 2004 film, *Anatomie d'enfer*. In Breillat's version the roles are inverted: a woman pays a homosexual man to accompany her on a four-day trip to explore the female body and sexuality. Both works have in common that the narrative unfolds in a place isolated from society, that the female protagonist is lying on a bed, and that the characters reject conventions, limits, and taboos to confront unnamable aspects of female sexuality. In a sense, in both novella and the film the characters wage a metaphysical battle of sexualized wills. Without becoming archetypes, what Duras's text reveals is the gap between the sexes that can sometimes be the abyss of torture due to the discontinuity between beings. While *Anatomie d'enfer* ends with a violent act, in Duras's novella there is no catharsis: the man seems not to have loved the woman. "You have never loved a woman? You say, no, never. She asks: You have never desired a woman? No, never." In *La Maladie de la mort*, love is death and the malady is also the romantic drive to transgress the limits toward and with the other. At the same time, the novella transmits a pessimistic vision of amorous realization of the heterosexual couple. When she wrote the novella, Duras was living with Yann Andréa, a homosexual who was thirty-eight years younger than her and with whom she shared her life until her death in 1996. To Duras, love is beyond a logic of sexual difference because love occupies the site of the irrational. What defines modern Western sensibility, moreover, is this form of passionate heterosexual love. Denis de Rougemeont describes love as an inexplicable link between death and impossibility.[3] Passion for him implies suffering, because it is a yearning that annihilates us as subjects when it triumphs over us. Passion always presupposes a third element that constitutes impossibility or an obstacle for love, be it social, moral, conventional, political; in *La Maladie de la mort* that third element is sexuality. Duras's novella posits the greatness of heterosexual love as something impossible to resolve due to irreconcilable sexual differences between man and woman. That is why heterosexual love is posited as an attempt toward the impossible repeated in every affaire: before it occurs, it is a lost love. And in Duras, the malady of death is also homosexuality because it implies the negation of the difference between the sexes and a form of love that is radically different than heterosexual love.

In *The Inoperative Community*, Maurice Blanchot takes Duras's novella as a point of departure to articulate his concept of "community."[4] For Blanchot, community is not a basis of shared values that makes meaningful forms of law that bind a group of people. For Blanchot, the law is always silent, unachieved, and it escapes the subject's comprehension. That is why a community disappears as it manifests itself. The hopeless love story in *La Maladie* is for Blanchot an archetype of a "community of lovers." The lovers are simultaneously isolated from the world and inaccessible to each other. As if death were standing between them, the unconventional nature of their relationship lacks the feeling of eternity or transcendence that characterizes community in Western secular nonnationalistic terms. In this way, the impossible love between a heterosexual woman and a homosexual man is posited by Blanchot as the archetype of an ethical relationship with an Other that neither assimilates to a cohesive, identitarian I or to a predetermined shared life, but implies absolute mutual responsibility. I know exactly why I am writing this, because I am dodging something I cannot yet write about.

Existential Eroticism and Modernism in Jeff Koons and Marcel Duchamp

The Nude Appearance at the Jumex Museum in Mexico City was an exhibition curated by Massimiliano Gionni bringing together artworks by Marcel Duchamp and Jeff Koons. While taking in the resonances established by the juxtaposition of artworks at the erotic-pornographic room of the show, I recalled feeling perplexity as I did when as a teenager I read Julio Cortázar's *Rayuela* (1963; *Hopscotch*) for the first time. The perplexity came from feeling unable to identify with La Maga, the novel's main female character: clumsy at maternity (she constantly neglects her son Rocamadour and lets him die of a cold) and null as an intellectual (she is always portrayed as the ignorant party listening to male erudite mansplaining), La Maga is like André Breton's *Nadja* (1928): an unpredictable, volatile, mysterious, and inscrutable, unreal! character with whom the lead male has hazardous encounters.[1] In a way, La Maga and Nadja are the opposite of a flesh and bone woman. In *Rayuela*, the encounters between La Maga and Oliveira, the main character, inevitably end up in casual sex in cheap hotels. The presence of La Maga in the novel is activated by the gaze of the man who desires her calling her into his presence to satisfy his own desire. This mechanism is similar to the way in which Nadja functions in Breton's novel, and to the female character of Juan García Ponce's novel and short story *El Gato*. In García Ponce, the female character is in a permanent state of sexual arousal, constantly undressing without provocation, desiring and being desired. To give you an idea of the mechanism that I sense operates in these female literary figures I will quote a fragment from *El Gato*:

> Every time D was alone reminiscing about her friend he imagined her like that, indolently extended on a bed, with sheets that could invariably cover her up but that were rejected as she slept, as she offered her body to contemplation in total abandonment, as if the only reason of her existence was to be admired by D because her body did not really belong to her, but to him, and perhaps also to the apartment's furniture and to the quiet branches of the trees on the street.[2]

I suspect that the source of inspiration for García Ponce's "her" was Octavio Paz's interpretation of *La Mariée* or the Bride from Duchamp's *Le Grand verre* (Great glass, 1917–1923)—hence the male character's name "D."[3] If we compare these female literary figures to the ones in the erotic-pornographic room at the Koons-Duchamp exhibition at the Jumex Museum, similarities begin to flourish, as they seem to embody an erotic mechanism that is not only archetypal but canonical in modern art history, literature, photography, and cinema.

In general, the juxtaposition of Marcel Duchamp and Jeff Koons's work awakens disquiet and polarization. On the one hand, Duchamp is conceived as the immaculate father of twentieth century modern art, while Koons's integrity is always questioned because of his relationship to the art market, for seemingly betraying the autonomy of art and for trivializing its content. Both artists have in common that they operate at the border between art and non-art, and from Duchamp to Koons we see a transition from the economy of the production of merchandise and consumption to the evolution of art into mass entertainment that justifies the banal, kitsch, and tasteless aspects of Koons's work.

The exhibition room in question is framed by a bracket constituted by a reproduction of *Le Grand verre, ou, La Mariée mise à nu par ses célibataires, même* (1917–1923; *The Great Glass, or, The Bride Stripped Bare by Her Bachelors, Even*) by Duchamp and by Koons' *Metallic Venus* (2010–2012), inspired by the Hellenistic sculpture known as *Venus Callipyge*. The room also includes Duchamp's *Le Bec auer* (1967), from his series of engravings of erotic and love scenes inspired by the history of art, and works from the series *Made in Heaven* by Koons (1990–91), which includes photographs of the artist in explicit sexual positions with La Cicciolina as model, along with mundane objects that make reference to baroque and rococo art history. We also find sketches from Duchamp's last installation, which took him twenty years to complete, *Étant donnés: 1° la chute d'eau, 2° le gaz d'éclairage* (1946–66; *Given: 1. The Waterfall, 2. The Illuminating Gas*) his three molds based on or allusive to genitals; and the photograph titled *Ciné-sketch: Adam and Eve*, which is a nude portrait of Duchamp and Bronia Perlmutter from 1924 taken by Man Ray. Koons and Duchamp are in obvious dialogue with the canonical conventions of art history regarding heteronormative representations of sexuality, appealing to the tradition of the representation of eroticism in modernity inaugurated by painters like Gustave Courbet, Édouard Manet, Auguste Rodin, and Jean-Auguste Dominique Ingres. Are they love, erotica, or porn narratives? Or do they contain elements from all three discourses or forms of representation?

The difference between eroticism and pornography is steep: both begin with nudity, that is to say, with an opening to the exterior. But while pornography is associated with the conscious contemplation of a sexual act beyond the reproductive function opposed to animal sexuality, eroticism, according to Georges Bataille, is characterized by the search for an external object of desire that responds to the interiority of desire. This is why the border between eroticism and pornography is not so thin: pornography is the repetitive and obsessive representation of the sexual act, eliminating imagination and seduction, which are also the basis for eroticism. While eroticism is subtle, pornography is an excess of reality of the sexual act. It seems like sexually explicit images have always existed, but pornography as a category of moral and legal classification is definitely a modern invention. The discovery of the Roman city of Pompeii in the nineteenth century inaugurated porn as a new category of sexually explicit images and objects lodged in an archive. The difference to approaches to this material before, after, and during modernity is that in Pompeii sexually explicit images and sculptures were not hidden but were part of other aspects of domestic and civic life. If in the nineteenth century pornography was invented by hiding sexually explicit images from the public gaze, their exposure as pornography would become a central characteristic of modernity.

Marcel Duchamp has been described as a "transcendental pornographer," while Jeff Koons's series *Made in Heaven* (1990), made in collaboration with porn actress Ilona Staller (also known as La Cicciolina), is directly pornographic. Pornography in both artists presupposes a kind of metaphysics of representation of Western and modern sexuality: a "truth" about sex that the image approaches or registers. If the erotic operates through a mise en scène of the dialectic between hiding and unveiling, the permanent presence of the pornographic visible destroys the imaginary: there is nothing to see but the ugliness of the sexual act. The title of the exhibition, *Nude*

Appearance, borrows its title from Octavio Paz's book about Marcel Duch-amp published in 1968. In his interpretation of *Le Grand verre*, Paz argues that the piece is the mise en scène of a myth, part of a family of myths related to the theme of the virgin and a closed masculine society grounded on the separation between the sexes and women's dependency on men. *Le Grand verre*, however, is one of the most hermetic artworks of the twentieth cen-tury. It is a "painting-text," accompanied by a box known as the *Boîte verte* full of notes describing the symbolic functioning of the enigmatic forms that we see suspended between the two sheets of glass. The notes reveal that the section above is inhabited by *La Mariée* (The Bride) isolated in her own world apart from the bachelors below her. The title of the artwork indi-cates an imaginary operation occurring in the painting: a disclosure, the exposure of the bride. This implies the idealization of the bride's sexuality, described as *épanouissement* or blooming. *Le Grand verre* is therefore an inventory of the elements of that blooming, of the imagined sexual life of the desiring-bride. Directed to orgasm, the *épanouissement* is nonetheless out of her reach because within the given conditions of the painting, it is impossible that she can get satisfaction. In Paz's interpretation, The Bride blooms, opens up, and dilates with pleasure. She doesn't reach orgasm but the sensation that precedes it. In sum, *Le Grand verre* is the image of the stripping bare of the bride, a striptease that is a spectacle, a ceremony, a mechanical operation, a physical-chemical process, the erotic experience of an engine whose fuel (that Duchamp calls "automobiline") is desire fed by electric discharges that awake the bachelors in the lower part. Accord-ing to Paz, the virgin brings the bachelors to life; all their activity, moreover, is a mixture of adoration and aggression toward her caused by the energy the Bride radiates and that is directed by her and toward her. That is why she is condemned to remain a virgin.

Duchamp's *Bride* is comparable to Koons's *Metallic Venus*: both are female figures in the process of exposing themselves; Duchamp's Bride undresses, driven by her own desire fed back to her through the bachelors in the lower part of the painting and by the "optical witnesses." Koons's *Venus* strips bare when activated by the viewer's gaze. The *Metallic Venus* is inspired by the Hellenic sculpture discovered in Naples in the nineteenth century known as the *Venus Callipyge*, which means in Greek "she of the beautiful buttocks." The *Venus Callipyge* embodies an instance of *anasyrma*, the gesture of pro-vocatively lifting her skirt to show her bare genitals or behind, a gesture that has been linked to religious rites, to eroticism, and to lascivious jokes. When the statue was discovered, her head was lost and the pose of looking over her shoulder to admire her behind, an attitude explicit to erotic exhibitionism, is the result of the restoration of the statue. A different angle of the head would take away the posture's narcissism and self-absorption, letting us see a woman displaying a beautiful body, as does Koons's *Metallic Venus*. While Duchamp's *Bride* exists in a hermetic, symbolic, and imaginary meta-world, Koons's *Metallic Venus* undresses directly for the viewer. According to philosopher Byung-Chul Han, the shine of Koons's sculptures reveals a characteristic trait of our contemporary societies: the elimination of the negative. For Han, the polished object invites the observer to cancel distance, emptying every object of sense and symbolism. The polish is sheer positivity and painless hedonism, without a wound or guilt, the sacralization of the banal. If negativity in art implies shaking and overturning the viewer, displacing her, creating distance, or shocking her, the positivity of Koons's polished molds sync up perfectly with the viewer, because the only thing the work seeks to do is to please, to elicit a "Like."[4] We can thus interpret the *Metallic Venus*'s shameless exhibitionism as the elimination of voyeuristic transgression: after seeing her, *anything can be seen*.

We should also consider that *The Bride*'s and *Venus*'s sexualities represent a state of permanent excitement that indefinitely postpones female pleasure. This form of representing femininity is a modern convention inaugurated by Édouard Manet who invented a new relationship between painting and viewer, incorporating the spectator into the painting's narrative. The viewer, however, is always masculine, his gaze interpellated by an object of desire. Manet's *Olympia* (1863) is already naked and aware that there is someone looking at her, as opposed to classic female nudes in the history of painting, in which nude women were depicted chastely because they are self-absorbed, unknowing that the viewer is present and looking at them. That is why in classical painting, differently from in modernity, there is no exhibitionism that can give way to the viewer's voyeurism, because the story or scene unfolds in a world apart. In the conventional modern nude, however, the spectator comes to embody the mechanism that structures the desire to look, sexualizing femininity in terms of male desire and gaze.

To return to my own perplexity at the beginning of the text, Where am I as a female spectator/reader in the erotic room at the Duchamp/Koons exhibition? I will remit to art historian Amelia Jones's narration of her encounter with *Étant donnés* when she was a student. From her feminist perspective, she is horrified. Something hinders her in solving her response to the piece; she is afraid of being seen, looking. The installation activates her female anger by tacitly making her participate in heteropatriarchy; she feels confusion and discomfort when sensing her own impulse of wanting to see an inert female body in a sexualized position according to the conventions of the representation of the female body in heteropatriarchal Western culture. Her discomfort results from the exaggeration in this posture and from Duchamp's strategy of placing the viewer (conceived as masculine) in the place of the voyeur. In this manner, *Étant donnés* leaves the female spectator in a site of displacement and dislocation. But when Jones, the feminist spectator, places herself in a masculine position that means to occupy the site of the mastery of vision proclaimed by heteropatriarchy, *Étant donnés*, she says, excites her homosexual desire.

When we as women place ourselves in the place of the mastery of vision from a masculine perspective, however, we are besieged by the rules and conventions of a predetermined masculine point of view. The consequence of observing female figures that exhibit sexual availability responding to the masculine desire they themselves elicit, we experience dislocation (even as lesbians). In these cases, the female body exists only to be valued as a sign of desire for men that the female body in itself lacks, transforming the image of the female into a masculine fantasy of a seducing femininity enabled by the consciousness of the desire she generates in men. Under this logic, masculine strength resides in producing, evidencing, revealing, while feminine power consists in seducing, retiring something from the order of the visible because the woman "holds" seduction, she is the center of attraction around which an erotic ritual in the imaginary world is inaugurated and originated. In this world, the feminine appears as a symbolic other who voluntarily subjects herself to eroticism: opened outward, limitless, she is an other that has in turn interiorized the other as she exteriorizes herself. In that way, female value and pleasure are reduced to functions of male desire and internalization of the masculine gaze. When women assume this structure of valorization, our autonomy is restricted: she is relegated to desiring being desired, and this is a form of coercion and the basis of the perpetuation of heteropatriarchy. Shay Welch has conceptualized this condition inherent to the regime of sexual difference as "existential eroticism." This regime remits women to sexual slavery, anchoring their beings on an aesthetic of seduction, the stylization of desire, and a choreography of pleasure. Again and again it is necessary to stress that this regime, far from being natural, is the historical construction of an aesthetic of domination that eroticizes and perpetuates gendered power differences.[5] These structures are the product of an epistemology that fixes definitions and the positions of men and women in the world, transforming bodies into sexualized social relationships.

In sum, pornography or the erotic representation in Duchamp and Koons is premised on the construction of a gaze that creates hierarchies and visual codes that designate something as "normal" or "transgressive." This gaze also normalizes sex between heterosexual couples in a romantic union (or not) from a site that naturalizes and presupposes (by erasure) the dislocation of my own gaze: as I refuse "existential eroticism," I am always absent from such an act.

In a way, women's identity (after hundreds of female characters in film, art, literature, television, and advertising is defined according to or in opposition to desire demanded and expected access by men to women's sexuality. Desiring and being desired, "the feminine" flourishes in an economy in which the most valuable trait of a woman is being beautiful and sexually desirable. In this manner, female identity is defined as *being* in relationship with or in resistance to masculine desire, as desirability legitimates the sense of the I and a woman's performance of femininity.

Elle, the main character of the eponymous movie by Paul Verhoeven (2016), is a representation of "existential eroticism" taken to the extreme. The film is about a phallic woman (Isabelle Huppert) seen from her neighbor's point of view, as someone who enjoys being subdued, violated, and raped over and over again by him. As Luis Buñuel's *Belle du jour, Elle* becomes the allegory of the internalization of an extreme version of the masculine fantasy of the desire to be possessed; in her case, by force. *Elle* embodies the tautology of being woman: "I raped you because you are a woman and you are a woman because I raped you." "Existential eroticism" is also the modus vivendi and operandi of the protagonist of Steven Soderberg's *The Girlfriend Experience* (2000), which tells the story of an escort who offers "experiences" of love relationships to her clients to whom she presents herself as submissive, pleasing, loving, sweet, and always willing. Another literary character that comes to mind in this context is the protagonist of Guadaulpe Nettel's short story "Hongos" (2013), which describes in the first person her extramarital affair with Philippe Laval, a married musician living in Belgium. Her desire and love for him lead her to stop living her life, her marriage is destroyed, and she only "feels alive" during the encounters orchestrated by Laval across the world. She isolates herself to such an extent that she tells us, "Our phone calls and virtual conversations became my only enjoyable contact with another human being." One day, she realizes that in the same way in which "love" sprang between her and Philippe, fungi manifested in her genitals. Instead of getting rid of them, she decides to embrace and cultivate them: she controls them, however, not letting them get close to her crotch. When her husband leaves her, she waits for Laval to call or look for her to see her. At the end, she becomes an invisible being plagued by fungi (an allegory of her desire) who only exists to desire and be desired by Philippe. During her wait to see him, she tells us, "I enjoy the darkness and the humidity of the walls. I spend many hours touching the cavity of my sex—that crippled pet that I saw in my childhood—where the fingers awaken the notes Laval has left imprinted on it."[6] The character falls short in taking back her own desire, and that is her doom.

A radical attempt to undo the male gaze and propose a female desiring gaze is Céline Sciamma's *Portrait de la jeune fille au feu* (2019; *Portrait of a Lady on Fire*). By telling a love story between two women, Sciamma's film seeks to undo the logic behind which the incarnation of masculine desire has been perpetuated as a feminine desiring figure. This situation is analogous to the masculine monopolization of the floor to speak while the feminine embodies the received word. This is nothing other than the misogynist, secularized Christian narrative of God the Father inseminating the Virgin Mary through her ear. According to me, Stan Brakhage's film *Window Water Baby Moving* (1959), in which we see beautiful images of the birth of Brackage's daughter edited in a progressive loop, is the only one, if not one of the few, art images in modernity in which the female body appears as a vehicle for the creation and life in the canonical Western History of art, possibly since the Willendorf Venus. We must include here a mention of Agnès Varda's *L'une chante et l'autre pas* (1977; *One Sings, the Other Doesn't*), a narrative about two women's feminist awakening and journey into appropriating their reproductive function, and a recent video installation made by Berlin-based artist Candice Breitz, *Labour* (2019). In this work, she addresses reproductive justice, female power, and global fascisms. *Labour* comprises four single-channel videos in a loop showing women giving birth in reverse. Each one of the videos is hidden behind a curtain and can be seen by one person at a time. Viewers had been warned of the disturbing nature of the visual material—which reinforces the intimate and taboo-like of representations of the female body giving birth. The logic behind Breitz's *Labour* is the possibility of undoing labor when reproductive justice is enacted or if men become tyrants and dictators.

An earlier attempt to take back our bodies and desires from modern canonical forms of female representation was by visual artist Hannah Wilke, who made in 1974 a performance in the Duchamp exhibition room at the Philadelphia Art Museum. She wore a white suit and a fedora hat to perform an act of autoeroticism to take back feminine desire and liberate Duchamp's *Bride* behind *Le Grand verre*. The dance was filmed through a shattered glass and the symbolic phallic and vaginal forms congealed in a union that remains unconsummated. The Bride and the bachelors will never be able to complete their task, but Wilke did, by becoming the active counterpart of *The Bride* in order to liberate her. Also exposed, she escaped the gaze of the ocular witnesses and the sparks coming in from the Bachelors from below. She thus took over control of her own exhibitionism, liberating herself from the masculine gaze.

Against "authoritarian modernity" that reaffirms sexual difference through the uneven distribution of desire and desirability, artist Sylvie Blocher created a last object in 2001: *La Mariée déçue, se rhabilla* (The bride, disappointed, gets dressed). In making this installation, Blocher decided to appropriate art as a utopian space for freedom by materializing the bride. In rendering her three dimensional, she ceases to be untouchable and lost in the milky way of *Le Grand verre*. Placed on the ground, Blocher's *Bride* exhibits her fragility. She carries within a light that shines underneath her veil and that can only illuminate her autonomously during eight hours a day: her energy is thus limited, but she has the ability to recharge herself. She also does not believe in God or in the authority of the fathers.

Wilke's performance and Blocher's installation are examples of earlier and very much needed feminist models to negotiate and expose the patriarchal forms of representation of women. Women's existential eroticism, or our existence as beauties and sexual objects for men, is rooted on the epistemology of objectivity as an ontological extension of the subject. That is why, following Paul B. Preciado, in order to dismantle heteropatriarchy we need an epistemological rupture grounded on categorical disapproval of the rapeability of women that would enable cognitive emancipation and the understanding that sex and sexuality are not ontological properties of the subject, but the product of an array of social and discursive technologies that administer truth and life.

In order to achieve a cognitive emancipation that would enable the epistemological rupture, it is necessary to abandon language and representations of sexual difference and identity. Also, to recognize that becoming woman is neither a fact or a biological destiny but a process that occurs through the corporealization of power: "I raped you because you are a woman and you are a woman because I raped you" is the tautology found at the center of the feminine experience. "Being woman" is the product of a social relation, political and ideological formation that denies that women are the product of exploitation and rape under heteropatriarchy. The unfortunate sequels of the #MeToo movement are a sign that the cognitive emancipation and epistemological rupture are urgent. What I have in mind here is the response of US vice president Mike Pence against the movement of denouncing the objectivization of women, which has been to inaugurate the tendency to oppose having meetings alone with a woman, hiring women for jobs that require a close relationship, or to hiring attractive women.[7]

To conclude, the juxtaposition of Duchamp's and Koons's work reveals that the mechanism of the "eroticism of things" is analogous to or stems from the existential eroticism attributed to the feminine mystique. Capitalism, which has transformed art into merchandise and subsumed all areas of life and human interaction to the market, is based on the libidinal economy, which implies the production and permanent externalization of desire that never achieves pleasure or satisfaction. It is urgent to liberate desire from existential eroticism and the libidinal economy, allowing ourselves to enjoy differently than consumption-based jouissance and beyond heteropatriarchal pre-established gender roles.

Postcard for *Historias Propias* (Stories of Our Own) by Lorena Wolffer

An experience which has marked me as being inhabited by or inhabiting gender is something that I was only able to begin to recognize when I could start to define myself as "queer." I realized that I had been conditioned my whole life to occupy the place of the passive object of seduction—perhaps leading me unconsciously to inhabit "existential eroticism," and that got me into a lot of trouble. I would let myself be seduced by men and get into relationships without really wanting to. My provincial, religious, repressive, and misogynist education had disabled me, turned me against my will. When I was coming out I had no idea if I should or could invite a girl out, if I should pay for her meal or drink? With time, I managed to break through the conditioning armor and I learned to seduce women instead of passively waiting to be seduced. And yes, the breakthrough required moving to a big city, crossing to the other side of the volcanoes, inhabiting a mirror image of the past where I could be myself.

In the new life, my daughter had to change schools because a commute to her old one was not an option. I had a long list of schools and was concerned about my daughter being discriminated against for being the daughter of a lesbian or for living in a homoparental family. I made phone calls to all the schools on my list asking the following questions: Do you have a spot for next school year for pre-first? What is your policy for homoparental families? The school next door invited me to visit, and I had a quite unpleasant conversation with the psychologist who demanded an explanation about a contradiction she perceived between "being a lesbian" and "being a mother" with a father who is present. I was deeply offended and crossed out the school as an option. I ended up enrolling my daughter in a school that has an explicit policy of tolerance to homoparental families. In spite of this policy, my daughter was placed in a group of children who are "other" or "nonnormative"—that is, foreigners. The other three groups in her grade host "normative" Mexican children. Ten years ago, gay marriage was legalized in Mexico City, but in spite of this legal measure, society is definitely not ready for it.

One day when I was leaving the house in a hurry, I quickly drove out of the garage and accidentally hit a blue car parked across the street. I left a few scratches on the car's body; mine was definitely worse off. I debated whether to write an apology and my phone number on a piece of paper to offer to fix the damage. I didn't do it partly because I was truly in a rush, partly for indolence, and partly as a gesture of vengeance for all the times my car has taken a hit without the damaging part taking responsibility. "This is the world we live in," I told myself. To make things worse, a few days later I realized that the car I hit parks every day near my house. Now, to justify my own indolence and cynicism, I live with the malicious fantasy that the car I hit belongs to the ignorant and offensive school's psychologist who interviewed me.

Perhaps my angry need for revenge stems from the excruciating years it took me to leave the closet due to my repressive, provincial education, but also because Mexico and its cultural world are still heteronormative. For instance, in *El vaquero del medio día* (*Midday Cowboy*, 2019), Diego Enrique Osorno's documentary about the damned poet Samuel Noyola doesn't even hint at the homosexual relation he had with Octavio Paz in the 1990s. The film, moreover, is focused on testimonies from his girlfriends who describe a typically toxic vanguardist masculinity. It goes without saying that Paz's bisexuality is taboo, as is the homosexuality of many Mexican writers. It is not surprising that the first lesbian novel in Mexico, *Amora* by Rosamaría Roffiel, was published as late as 1989. And the fact that the pioneer of human and civil rights for homosexuals and lesbians in Mexico is not Carlos Monsiváis, but Nancy Cárdenas, is not so well known.

As the story is told, when Nancy Cárdenas came out of the closet one Sunday in 1973 on public television on Jacobo Zabludovsky's show, defending the human and civil rights of the LGBT+ community and criticizing homophobia—the community had always been subject to *redadas,* or raids in which homosexuals would be temporarily arrested by the police, among other forms of discrimination—she was condemned by other intellectuals and writers who scorned her for making her sexuality public. But the day after coming out of the closet on national television, she and Monsiváis went out to have lunch at a restaurant in the then fashionable Zona Rosa, and people came up to congratulate and thank her. At the time, people associated with the Right disseminated posters with her portrait identifying her as "Mexico's enemy." Nancy experienced censorship, persecution, and harassment for being publicly a lesbian; she took her provocateur reputation with a good sense of humor and carelessness, and her activism was not limited to fighting for the rights of homosexuals and lesbians. In the 1970s she wrote a manifesto against gay raids, "En contra de las razzias," censored by the many magazines she pitched it to until Monsiváis published it in the cultural supplement of *¡Siempre!* Today our most visible lesbian referents circulate in the celebrity world, from Sarita García to Montserrat Olivier. There is also Cecilia Fuentes. And although we do not appear as stereotypes in telenovelas as gay men do, we are slowly and steadily acquiring more visibility and respect in public space, thanks to pioneer fighters like Nancy.

The Pencil of Nature and Other Appropriations

The Pencil of Nature is a series of female portraits by Yvonne Venegas as well as the title of William Henry Fox Talbot's treaty on photography. Talbot's experiments with the *camera obscura* are precursors of the art and technology of photography. Delivered in six parts between 1844 and 1846, Talbot's *The Pencil of Nature* is a detailed history of the technique of the art of making images with light and silver nitrate and includes a selection of the first twenty-four photographs ever made. Back then, viewers were surprised by the likeness of the origin or cause of the image, which was created by "chemical writers" without an artist's hand or human intervention. The main effect of "photogenic writing," in other words, was the absolute veracity of the image, complete in detail and correct in perspective, achieved through direct contact and impression on the photographic paper. Yvonne Venegas's appropriation of the title of Talbot's treaty is an ironic gesture for a series of portraits that question "the feminine" as a quality conferred by nature and photography as a true register of its cause. In that manner, one of the series' goals is to break with the myth of the image objectively registering nature to underscore the intervention of the gaze in the photographic act, and how the image is always framed by the relationships between the looker and who is looked at. It goes without saying that gender is also at stake in a photographic exchange of gazes and central to Venegas' experiment for the series.

Venegas' point of departure for *The Pencil of Nature* is to quote or remake classic female portraits framed by masculine gazes from the canonical history of photography. In some of the images women are thus photographed

in angles and poses recognizable from images by the "great masters," allegedly the "origin" of the art of photography. It must be mentioned that some
of the women portrayed by Venegas work with their bodies for a living,
that is to say, their jobs require a high degree of bodily awareness and control: acting, yoga, modeling. Another section of the series is comprised by
images in which Venegas portrays herself imitating self-portraits by the
"great masters," taking the double role of being seen and being author. A
third section of the series consists of remakes of classic modern portraits
of women by male photographers.

Venegas' appropriations are reminiscent of conceptual artist Sherrie
Levine, who at the end of the 1970s questioned the role of the romantic artist-
genius by appropriating key modernist works, on the one hand, to decon-
struct their fetishization by the history of art that links creation to masculine authorship and gaze considered as "genius" and "authentic." Levine
created almost identical copies of images and works by male authors, for
instance, in her series *After Walker Evans: 1–4* (1981). On the other hand,
the gesture of copying and replicating artworks by males, in Levine as in
Venegas, can be read as a feminist critique against heteropatriarchy in the
history of art and society. How can women appropriate creativity, as it is
considered to be a masculine attribute? What is the role of the feminine
gaze? Does it have a place in the contemporary world? Beyond the sexu-
alization and essentialization of women by the traditional male gaze, Can
we really tell the gender of gaze?

The series of female portraits and self-portraits by Venegas also takes
up the historical issue of the masculine gaze as having constructed certain
forms of femininity and masculinity through frames of gestures and poses
allegedly witnessing a "natural" or "essential" femininity. That is to say, the
history of canonical photography is plagued by instances in which photographers have used the body and female identity to objectify and sexualize
women, generating pleasure through the gaze. This was achieved by portraying women assuming gestures of "desirability" from the masculine point of
view, with submissive poses and gestures, flirtatious looks, infantilization,
or vulnerability. The masculine gaze has traversed us historically without
asking, male photographers erasing women from their portraits. As we
know, however, the "naturalness" of the feminine perpetuated through the
visual codes of modern photography is a discursive construction, because
the body is not a "mute fact" of nature, but the reproduction of predetermined discourses about gender. That is to say, there are no "natural bodies"
that pre-exist the cultural inscription of gestures, which as a whole confer
"truth effects" on sexual identity. Sexual identities, as photographs, are "con-

structions" and not natural effects. Therefore, if a photograph is an image constructed by an interplay of gazes, gender is the performance of certain codes of gender identities and given corporeal styles.

From this point of view, Yvonne's portraits are an interrogation of the normative gestures of femininity and masculinity built by the masculine gaze by changing the terms of the traditional relationship between "photographed" and "photographer." Underscoring the fact that desire also comes into play in the act of portraiture (the desire to see and the desire to be seen), Yvonne experiments with forms of portraying women: first, through self-portraiture imitating the "masters," by restaging photographs of "male geniuses" by famous photographers, like the photo of PJ Harvey by Helmut Newton (with a gun in her mouth), a photograph of Diane Arbus by Norman Mailer, a portrait of Juan Rulfo by Manuel Álvarez Bravo and finally, a self-portrait by Malick Sidibe. In two photographs of the series, she does remakes of Erwin Blumfeld's portrait with his face covered with paper.

For the female portraits from the series, Venegas builds exchanges of gazes that give way to the assertion of the identities of the women portrayed, transmitting a kind of beauty and femininity that are not necessarily conditioned by the sexualized and pre-established repertoire of gestures and poses from the canonical modern masculine gaze. Photographing friends and women with whom she establishes friendship ties, Yvonne gives way to playful interaction, allowing the women to show themselves as they are/ wish to be seen, freeing themselves (or not) from the burden of a sexualized and prewritten sexualized "femininity." In that manner, the female portraits of the series *The Pencil of Nature* break and renegotiate the codes of femininity and masculinity of the "originary" photographs. Venegas achieves this through complicities and ties that are different than sexualized ones, desexualizing the desire to be seen and to see.

For a masterclass at the Toronto International Film Festival (TIFF) in 2016, director Joey Soloway delivered their theory of the feminine gaze, which in practice is not far from Yvonne's experiments. They define the masculine gaze as an energy triangle that comes from three points that interconnect to objectify women: the person behind the camera, the person portrayed, and the spectators. That is why Soloway gave themself the task to build a feminine gaze departing from the same three elements, seeking to recuperate the feminine body, to attract and return the gaze. For Soloway, the female gaze includes how women feel, see, and experiment with being looked at by the opposite sex. Becoming conscious of the feeling of being seen is achieved through a subjective camera that tries to merge with the protagonists. Instead of simply gazing at the character, Soloway uses the frame to evoke the feeling of the sensation of being looked at with the purpose of creating empathy. For that, it is necessary that the camera person is conscious of his or her own body and able to transmit what Soloway calls "feeling/seeing." Aside from formally creating specifically female imagery, the female gaze also implies reclaiming the body to communicate the "feeling/seeing" and to become a tool to consciously create empathy.[1]

One day Yvonne came over for lunch to tell me about this project and to take my own portrait. I felt that it was my chance to experiment with becoming an image, something that's not easy for me because I have issues with bodily and spatial awareness (due in part to sensory processing disorder and in part, lack of confidence and shyness). During the photography session, I was hyperaware of the fact that I was by far not master of my own image! The other models Yvonne had worked with are women whom, as I mentioned, work with their bodies as a profession. I evidently tend to live inside my head all the time, and it is very hard for me to connect with my body, let alone to be able to project anything through my body language or facial expression. During the photography session, which was very fun because Yvonne has a lightness and a wonderful sense of humor that are contagious, we were talking about things, in relationship to her project but also about banal stuff. During the session, I was very confused in trying to pose before her camera; at moments I felt very comfortable, but when I remembered that I had to "be an image," I posed with a feeling of fear of falling into this readymade grammar of gender codes. But I also felt lost, without knowing how to "place myself," until a comment by Yvonne would make me laugh and the session would naturally continue. We were very pleased with the result.

Venegas's series *The Pencil of Nature* was exhibited at the Galería de Arte Mexicano in Mexico City simultaneously as "Días únicos: El estudio y su archivo" (Unique days: The studio and its archive), at the Museo Universitario Arte Contemporáneo (MUAC; University Museum of Contemporary Art, at the UNAM). The MUAC exhibition is also based on the appropriation of "originary images," in that case, of photographs from the archives of José Luis Venegas, owner of the Estudio Venegas in Tijuana and father of Yvonne Venegas. For this exhibition, Yvonne reread the 1970s archives of wedding photographs from the Estudio Venegas. The photographer's father documented weddings based on the classic formula of "twenty-five important moments": The bride putting an earring on, arranging her veil before the mirror, the groom and bride eating cake, et cetera. Studio wedding photographs, in other words, register a vocabulary of gestures and moments previously written in a script that eliminates the spontaneity in order to represent aspirational conventions

FIGURE 12. Yvonne Venegas, *Retrato Ausente (after Manuel Alvarez Bravo)* from the series *The Pencil of Nature* (2019), courtesy of the artist.

and social codes (including gender roles) of a middle class then in construction in Tijuana. The shots Yvonne selected from her father's archive combine photographs of the twenty-five important moments with images that were never printed to become part of the wedding album because they deviate from the norms of the social contract that wedding images are determined by. As a whole, the "unique moments" register a vocabulary of roles, gestures, poses, and characters that are eloquent about the perpetuation of a material culture and construction of a social class (waiters or others devoted to service are cut out from the wedding albums, for instance). Gestures and poses, moreover, are conditioned by repetition and become more or less unconscious, perpetuating a kind of "figurative behavior" in people portrayed that cannot be dissociated from language or communication. Beyond the photographed subject being conscious of becoming images, the "unique moments" reflect reality through gestural symbols translated to material forms of social conventions. At the same time, they register infra-verbal moments of visual behavior, communicating through the physical material of the body conventions transmitted through repetition and coercion. That is why Yvonne's intervention in her father's archive interrupts normative "figurative behavior" to disorganize the representation of social codes revealing the aspect and function of photography as a social contract and the construction (and not naturalness) of social and gender conventions.

The exhibition *The Pencil of Nature* concludes with the three-dimensional mise en scène of a photograph by Manuel Álvarez Bravo, *Retrato ausente* (1945; Absent portrait). In the original photograph, we see a woman's dress carefully arranged on a chair framed by an aura of light that enters diagonally from a window. Yvonne's three dimensional remake of the image shows a man's suit arranged on a chair adorned with a pocket watch. If from the feminist point of view we could read the absence of the female body, which in Álvarez Bravo's photograph results from the absolute idealization of woman, in Yvonne's remake, the absence of the body—which is a body codified as androgynous, because Yvonne wears the suit in one of her portraits—it denotes that gender, aside from being a construction, is a series of codes that can be appropriated and deconstructed. It also denotes the inescapability of the body's materiality, of the truth of biological sex, as the interior of the watch attests to because it contains traces of the artists' last menstruation. According to Simone de Beauvoir, menopause is the beginning of the ideal state of a woman: a third sex, liberated from the burden of sexual difference and offering the possibility of becoming a third gender, beyond the duality imposed by the social conventions of heteropatriarchy.

Cosmopolite Postcard

Walking across the streets of China Town in New York toward e-flux's head-quarters (Grand and Broadway), but also earlier at the airport during the long wait to pass through passport control, I am reminded of Mexico's monoculturality, and of how good it feels to circulate in this multicultural texture. In one block there is a Kosher meat shop administered by an Orthodox Jewish man, next to a Chinese electronics store run by a Latina, then a convenience store with an Arab young man at the cashier. The whole world is concentrated on the streets of New York, political and racial prob-lems are momentarily suspended in the interactions of daily life. Perhaps Mexico was like this long ago, during the Spanish colony era? Back then, Filipinos, Spaniards, Africans, Arabs, Jews, Indigenous Mexicans coexisted. Aside from predictable social tensions generated by the caste hierarchy, what would everyday interaction have been like between a "pure" Spaniards, "converted" Jews, Indigenous people, mestizos, Africans, Asians? Would there have been a moment in which the various cultural textures coexisted without being interwoven into a homogenous tapestry of food, language, and dress codes, as in certain areas of contemporary New York? After the presentation, we move to a bar where "Israeli" food is served. The tables are mostly occupied by white people like me, I suppose. I feel like a foreigner but also like I am part of something bigger than me: a global network of ideas, sentient and thinking beings existing together and linked; my inter-nal world makes sense beyond my here and now. The rest of the world is the source of the breath of my thinking articulated in written words.

Narcissism, Human Rights, and Postimperialist Utopias

The justification for burning the Amazon jungle by the Paraná ranchers in Brazil is narcissism. Narcissism is ubiquitous and perpetuates Social Darwinism as the main structure of neoliberal subjectivities and relationships. In order to grasp the selfishness of others, we must understand that its origin lies in the impossibility of being able to imagine occupying a different place than the one we already occupy in the world. Narcissism hinders us from being able to place ourselves in the shoes of others. We are trapped within ourselves, feeling self-sufficient and glorifying autonomy, thus nothing can displace a narcissist from the center of the world he/she is stuck in.

The narcissist script has created "heroes-victims" in film and TV series. For instance, *La camarista* (2019; The chambermaid) by Lila Avilés observes the life of a young mother centered on her work as a chambermaid in a luxury hotel in Mexico City. The heroine is a victim of a system that exploits her, but she is also the shero of her own life because she lives her Calvary with stoicism, aspiring to better herself: Eve (Gabriela Catrol) studies every night to pass the exams to get a middle school certificate, and she works very hard to earn the right to clean the next floor higher in the hotel where she works, which comes with a higher salary. *La camarista* makes visible a form of labor that is normally unseen, and the film leaves the viewer with a feeling of hope about Eve's future. A comparison to Luis Buñuel's *Los olvidados* (1950) or Chantal Ackerman's *Jean Diehlman* (1976) are beside the point, because what Avilés' films express is not the ordeal of the working or the marginal class but the market need to represent perfect neoliberal subjects who are victims of the system but heroes of their own lives—in the viewer's eyes they are thus not oppressed, because emancipation is seemingly in their own hands.

Narcissism is also a trait of a whole generation living their lives half time online, executing minor performances of an imagined celebrity, disseminating images, mini-memories, and diary entries looking at the world as a mirror of themselves, without having to show the least interest in others or in the future. The HBO series *I May Destroy You* (2020) by and starring Michaela Coel is a recent example: it is a story set in contemporary London about a young woman who is an emergent literary figure who must put up with the pressure of her agent and editor to produce a new book while dealing with the sequels of sexual abuse. Arabella, the shero/victim, flees the pressure, denial, anxiety, and pain by compulsively hiding behind her own celebrity image, constantly feeding her Instagram stories that posit her as a victim of the abuse while making shallow pseudofeminist declarations that she believes are empowering. Conveying superficial values and becoming vacuous referents—Arabella gains a lot of followers by exposing her ordeal—the role celebrities and influencers have in our societies is nothing other than a symptom of deep inequality producing the idolization of superiors (or the strongest in Darwinist terms), giving them a predominant place in our collective imaginaries. What is symptomatic is that these narcissist sheroes are the referents of feminist struggle, as opposed, for instance, to *bad* women who vindicate women's right to be violent, like Alia Trabucco's or Susana Vargas' old lady killer.[1]

Under the narcissistic illusion, others are fake and only the "I" is real. Could we imagine a politics or forms of postimperialist solidarity in the context of systemic narcissism at a global scale? First we would need to be wary of narcissism in leadership, of the heroic individual with messianic, individualist, macho tendencies (Duterte, Erdogan, Trump, Bolsonaro, Modi, López Obrador). Then we would have to invent alternatives to these leadership figures, bearing in mind that the male dictator is no longer exclusive to the so-called Third World and that they are governing by stirring passions as opposed to consciousness, reason, and debate. An alternative leadership would be collective, empathic, ruling by obeying, for instance (although López Obrador already appropriated this Zapatista slogan for his own government and it now sounds cliché). Leaders, thinkers, reference figures are needed, moreover, as horizontality in social movements has gotten us nowhere.

In a recent online conversation about postimperialist solidarity, Angela Davis stated that we assume the fact that the figure of the leader should correspond to a masculine notion of individualism and thus to messianic heroism, but in the era of Black Lives Matter, not only are women assuming leadership, but young activists are exploring different governance paradigms such as collective leadership. For Davis, it is key to get rid of the masculine ideal of the hero and to assume that leaders undergo pain and traumas. As opposed to leaving their past behind—as guerrilleras did, by leaving everything behind to embrace revolutionary struggle—the new leadership embraces empathy and self-care practices.[2] But above all, as I mentioned earlier, it is necessary to take a critical stand against the tools, concepts, vocabularies, and practices of contemporary political organization that characterize struggle landscapes by embracing and transcending the paradox that the tools we currently have to change the structures of an unfair system are inherited from that system. In other words, one of the problems we face in imagining a postimperialist politics is that the instruments we have to change the unjust structures that rule the world have been inherited from colonialism and materialized in the Nation-State and its institutions. We are dealing with the contradiction of trying to fight inequality and neocolonialism with illuminist values like human rights and education for everyone, which are values channeled by institutions that have justified or invisibilized dispossession at the global level in the first place. What alternative could there be to fight for land, food, and water when the State apparatus is not able to guarantee these basic human rights? When the demand that human rights be granted is narcissistic in principle?

In a posthumous book, one of my favorite philosophers, Simone Weil, made a critique to the human rights declared after the French Revolution. She explains that the problem with the State apparatus as guarantor of equality is that a right is only effective in relation to an obligation it corresponds to. When a right is guaranteed by the State, it is not effective because the State represents an abstraction apart from obligations. For Weil, therefore, the effective exercise of a right does not reside in an individual who possesses and reclaims rights from the State, but rather, rights are granted by other human beings who feel an obligation toward the individual. Positing the State as the guarantor of rights does not make any sense because rights and obligations are not distinct from each other.[3] An isolated or narcissistic person, however, only has duties toward herself, and from her point of view, she has rights but not obligations toward others. The problem is that if people are not bound by identical obligations executed in different manners according to particular circumstances, people demanding rights and reciprocity to the abstraction that is the Nation-State do so from a narcissistic point of view. In a recent conversation with Dawn Paley, we discussed the "Failed State," a concept that has been widely used in the media to describe the "hollowing out" of the neoliberalized State through privatizations and the apparent loss of national sovereignty due to "organized crime." According to Dawn, however, in perpetuating cycles of State violence, the State is not failed, rather, it has failed its citizens. Could it be that in so far as "the Nation-State" is an abstraction, a collectivity of narcissists is systematically failing itself?

For Simone Weil, in the realm of human relationships, the object of any obligation is the human being as such. Obligation exists toward each human being for the sake of *being* a human being; obligation is not based on any right: not on the law, habits and customs, social structure, power relations, or social inheritance. No fact from empirical reality can create an obligation toward others. Obligations are furthermore not based on conventions, because they get modified according to the historic and cultural context. The forms of obligations toward others described by Weil are tied to the *eternal destiny* of human beings. That is why duties toward other human beings are unconditional and founded not on something that is part of the material world, but rather on something that gets verified in the common agreement of universal human consciousness. For Weil, to not let others suffer is an eternal obligation connected to our moral right beyond human beings' vital needs listed as protection against violence and access to clothing, sanitation, and medical attention—formerly fulfilled by the welfare state.

Aside from the fact that an "eternal obligation" to someone is a joke for the narcissist, nowadays we conceive human rights very differently than Weil: guaranteeing rights has been transferred to the State apparatus. Rights sanctioned by the Nation-State, however, are being put at the service of certain objectives. For instance, education has the purpose of producing subjects with tools and knowledges that enable them to participate in an efficient manner in global capitalism. We urgently need a different form of education, a decolonizing kind, but the State will not provide for such an education. Granting minimum income for "the poor" through President Andrés Manuel López Obrador's Bienestar program, for instance, serves the purpose of incorporating "the poor" into the market as consumers. In this context, we also should rethink the principles of democracy, which in its neoliberal version has been structured to assimilate and consider minorities but with the sole purpose of allowing the capitalist machinery to keep on working smoothly, perpetuating racism in covert and not so covert forms. The perpetuation of racism by democracies is one of the reasons minorities do not feel represented by environmental crisis-led movements or why urban dwellers have difficulties in seeing the ordeals and understanding the struggles in rural areas for the defense of the territory.

It would also be interesting to find ways to liberate the State from its power to grant justice. I am not vouching for communal lynching, but rather, to put on the table the problem that the State holds the monopoly on violence while creating an industrial prison complex and militarizing the country, reproducing social and political forms of violence that serve neoliberal interests. In her recent book *Guerra neoliberal: Desaparición y búsqueda en el norte de México* (2020; Neoliberal war: Disappearance and search in the north of Mexico), Dawn Marie Paley argues that what is known as the "War against Drugs" is a form of expanded counterinsurgency in which paramilitary groups (State or nonstate agents) perpetrate crimes against vulnerable populations throughout Mexico, giving the state and corporations power through social cleansing.[4] In this context, civil society makes demands from the standpoint of victims seeking State restitution and justice. But in principle, the neoliberal State will never do justice, because the neoliberalization of the Nation-State implied eliminating the barriers between global capital and the State to serve the interests of oligarchs and transnational corporations in a world in which the majority of wealth (80 percent) is concentrated in a few hands (1 percent). The State now has more power than ever and according to Dawn, war is inseparable from neoliberalism.

Evidently, the model of the nineteenth-century bourgeois State is obsolete as is the pact that founded it, which implied administering the commons for the benefit of all of the (imagined) members of a nation, united in a territory through shared symbols, histories, and myths. Paradoxically, we need to protect and treasure "citizenship," although the Nation-State manages populations differentially: while the privileged populations are treated as citizens with rights, the redundant populations are treated as noncitizens and disposable populations, subject to social cleansing and unprecedented levels of State violence. But is it possible to imagine something different from the institution of the Nation-State, which can only guarantee the rights and well-being of a minority?

I suspect that the Nation-State in its neoliberal-corporate version is here to stay for the medium to long term, so perhaps a mid-term solution to our problems would be to bring into the political arena topics that are not necessarily part of it. I have for instance in mind the feminist initiative in the 1980s to struggle and lobby to change legislation and protect the sexual and reproductive rights of women, which until then had been demands outside of the law. Now they changed from being "women's problems" to urgent topics in the legislative national agenda. We need to gather teams of lawyers, activists, and creative people to demand to amend the law to grant food, water, and land for all beyond the useless frame of the human rights,

FIGURE 13. Lynn Umlauf, *January 20 1984*, photo by Adam Reich, courtesy of the artist.

to counter the loopholes created by neoliberal amendments to the law that have been used to privatize access to these basic rights.

Thinking about how urgent all of this is, I can't imagine what post-imperialist solidarity would look like if not led by Palestinians sharing their experiences of fifty plus years of resistance against apartheid, repression, occupation, and dispossession and by originary populations who could teach us how solidarity networks can be interwoven at the local and community levels. Their strategies would be much more effective than the abstract mass conformed by "civil society" navigating digital polarization and violence on the Internet.

We should also think about what our public worlds currently look like: in public worlds a space for appearance is constructed in common and for the collective. Our actual public worlds are now open to unheard of levels of vengeance, violence, and brutality. Bearing this in mind, for a postimperialist solidarity, we need young people to demand that adults in positions of power and privilege in relationship to capital, industry, and fossil fuels, mining, finance, the State—in brief, extractivism—make themselves responsible for climate change and its effects and stop holding on to their privileges, which are neither sustainable at the short or medium term: the cost is too high.

In a recent online conversation Arundhati Roy and Naomi Klein discuss the possibilities of international (or global) solidarity in the context of the COVID-19 pandemic and massive environmental catastrophe. For Klein, a Marshall plan for Planet Earth is required, starting by recognizing the debt owed from the North to the South in terms of carbon footprint that originated in colonialism. Then, Klein argues, we need to move from a logic of extractivism and disposable populations to a logic of care and repair of the Earth and one another, spreading awareness of the fissures and injustices that led us to the situation of the Coronavirus pandemic, inextricable from the climate crisis. This crisis, according to Klein, has put us into a situation in which the redundant (or sacrificial) populations are now considered "essential workers," as opposed to the sectors of the population who can afford the luxury of isolation. What is the role of those who are not essential to the economy? I think that the pandemic has put in front of us the need to move beyond our role as consumers and producers toward a re-evaluation of the role of reproduction in the sustainability of ourselves and humanity.

To think about a new international/global solidarity we need to start where the World Social Forum left off, putting on the table the fact that the Left failed and that we have a psychotic relationship to earth and to other human beings, that the enemies are corporations and the Right, and that the dynamics of capitalism make us very vulnerable, especially because supply chains are centralized and countries are lacking food autonomy. We must also refuse to normalize our "new normal" under the COVID-19 pandemic, resisting as much as we can the transubstantiation of education, work, and social relationships to interaction via screens.

The world we need to build needs thus to be founded on cherishing everyone (as opposed to treating people as disposable) then redefining the meaning of progress and civilization. In this context, international solidarity means sharing resistance tactics to counter populist leaders' means of disciplining the population, learning resistance strategies and failures from each other. To imagine a radical future together, we have to stand by the people who are taking the risks right now, doing the "essential jobs," defending their lands and livelihoods, being the victims of State violence. A political movement for a postimperialist world needs to encompass inequality, dispossession, and anticapitalism and invent strategies to flee from sites of capitalist extraction, having as its main goal decommodifying land, food, and water.[5]

Palestine Today

I met Kata at the Rosario Castellanos Library on September 11, 2019, after a public discussion on the political situation of Palestine. Kata is a beautiful jazz dancer from Hungary who has been living in Mexico for many years. After my talk, she introduced herself to me and we continued the discussion on the Israeli-Palestinian conflict. She also told me her father is an employee at the Szechenyi baths in Budapest, and that she spent her whole childhood there. I told her that those baths were special to me because that is where I went during a long layover of a flight from Israel back to Toronto, after having spent a long time (over a year) in the West Bank. On the way from Canada to Israel, I visited the Gellert Baths with O, an Israeli I befriended on the flight who had gone to Canada to try his luck and was planning to move his family there, because he was clear that he didn't want his children to serve in the army—he had seen and done terrible things during the Second Intifada and wanted his kids to grow up in another country. During that first stop in Budapest, I felt a mix of excitement for what awaited me and paranoia that O would find out that my final destiny was not Tel Aviv but Ramallah. I was scared that he would not take lightly my plan to spend many months in the Occupied Territories and that his reaction might jeopardize my trip. Months later, when I finally told him where I was, he took it better than I had expected. Later on, he would ultimately move his family to a suburb in Ontario.

More than a year after my stop in Budapest on my way to Tel Aviv, I chose to visit the Szechenyi baths while waiting for my flight back to Toronto. The constructions to enjoy thermal waters there date from the Baroque era and comprise a huge open space with interconnected circular pools. I spent as many hours as I could there, "decompressing," feeling on my flesh for the first time in many months the sadness of living (with privileges) the Palestinians' ordeal. At the baths, I realized I had been having trouble breathing for a long time, and the openness of the baroque space felt like a soul exfoliation. It was a nice coincidence to get to know Kata, as if the encounter had been an invitation to rethink how things have changed for the worse in the geopolitical situation of the conflict.

September 11 is the anniversary of a breakthrough event that ended the multicultural romance that used to veil the neocolonial project behind globalization. After the Twin Towers attacks in New York, the twenty-first century began with a wave of Islamophobia. After clashes between religious and cultural fundamentalism, we saw new forms of authoritarianism and fascism emerge across the world. At the same time, a new era of wars and permanent states of exception was inaugurated (some of them justified by ethnic conflicts), hiding a global wave of accumulation by dispossession and territorial control for the destruction of the commons (or extractivism). Before that conjuncture, the Israeli-Palestinian conflict had been the prototype and laboratory of war, dispossession, and redundant population control technologies of this century. Bearing in mind the fact that the Palestinian struggle constitutes a major imperial axis for controlling the rest of the world, without a doubt the occupation of Palestine and Zionism have ideological, religious, and strategic control stakes for imperialist elites.

The year 2020 marks seventy-two years since the Nakba, the catastrophic destruction of historical Palestine. It is also the fifty-third year of apartheid, uninterrupted military siege, dispossession, and systematic oppression as well as movement restrictions for Palestinians. We can add to this the ceaseless destruction of the Palestinians' social tissue along with their communal networks for subsistence and survival; their political structure, territorial sovereignty, infrastructure, and economic autonomy; their family networks; and their psychological well-being. These forms of destruction are taking place through extralegal extortion, torture, and corruption, and by means of subtle and not-so-subtle Israeli policies and laws: the Israeli State apparatus governs Palestinians alongside Israelis with a different set of rights, or rather, as noncitizens (without rights). An example of collective extortion and torture is the fact that in only a few cases does Israel allow Palestinians to leave the West Bank or Gaza for medical reasons; there are many cases of ill babies and children that have been hospitalized alone in Israeli healthcare institutions because Israeli authorities make it difficult for parents to accompany the minors. Just in 2018, fifty-six babies from Gaza were separated from their parents, six of whom died without any family members present.[1] The separation of children from their parents as a strategy of collective torture sounds familiar and can be linked to Donald Trump's punitive migration policy that separates migrant children from their parents, putting the former in refugee camps as the latter are deported. This is not mere coincidence, as Israeli Prime Minister Benjamin Netanyahu is somehow Trump's predecessor: In 2012, Netanyahu's government approved the "law of the prevention of infiltration" that decrees the automatic detention of anyone entering Israel without a permit, including asylum seekers. Many of these noncitizens are detained in concentration camps in the Negev desert, as in the Immigration and Customs Enforcement (ICE) centers across the United States.

Another Israeli policy designed to mortify Palestinians is to refuse to return to Palestinian families the bodies of their dead beloved ones who perished in combat against Israel. In August 2019, an open act of aggression and irresponsibility was perpetrated when Israeli forces shot tear gas, sound grenades, and rubber bullets at the Al-Aqsa Mosque while Muslim Palestinians gathered for the first day of Eid-al-Adha (the celebration of Sacrifice, the most important festivity in Islam). Dozens of Palestinians were injured in the attack; the clashes continued when Israeli authorities allowed hundreds of religious Jews to enter the sacred Al-Aqsa Mosque during Eid. On July 22, at the Wadi Hummus neighborhood in the outskirts of East Jerusalem, many families were expelled from their beds in the middle of the night and were forced to see the army destroy their homes. This form of expulsion and dispossession is also seen in Mexico. I am thinking about the incident in La Malinche in 2010. La Malinche is a popular neighborhood in the Magdalena Contreras borough in Mexico City, where the destruction of people's homes was justified by "taking over space" to build the Supervía Poniente (West Superhighway). The neighbors organized to resist the destruction of their homes, so a police operation "with legitimate use of force" was deployed against them. They were attacked again in November 2012 when grenadiers and Caterpillar trucks charged against the people and the camp Frente Amplio Contra la Supervía Poniente (Wide Front against the West Superhighway) they had erected in 2010.

The destruction of Palestinian homes by Israelis is so common that the Wadi Hummus incident I described would not have transcended to the international news if it weren't that this East Jerusalem neighborhood is under the control of the Palestinian Authority and the event was a clear territorial violation of Palestinian autonomy (granted in principle by international law). The recurrence of incidents like in Wadi Hummus illustrates that one of the aspects of the conflict is a demographic and real estate war that creates refugees. It is also well known that Palestinian children are regularly arbitrarily arrested, prosecuted, and detained by the army and the police to be subjected to physical and verbal violence, humiliation, painful physical coercion, death threats, sexual assault against them or their family members, and restricted access to the toilet, water, or food. Recently, the Knesset approved a law for "authorities of the occupation" to have the power to take the right to residence away from Jerusalem Palestinians if they "break their alliance with Israel."

All these systemic forms of injury, torture, and extortion impede the normal development of Palestinians, who live under what they call "the tyranny of incertitude," continuously subject to more repression and torture; in March 2018, Palestinians from Gaza began to demonstrate against the Israeli siege every Friday by the wall that separates the Strip from Israel. The army responded to Palestinians armed with stones and homemade grenades and bombs with fire directed at their legs to contain them. Thousands were wounded, and of the 10,500 treated in Gazan hospitals and clinics, at least 60 percent were wounded in the legs; 175 Palestinians died in the clashes. This wave of violence in 2018 left a visible mark in Gaza, where now youth are seen walking on the destroyed streets aided by crutches; at least 1,700 of the wounded ended up with amputations due to infections or because they required complex surgeries for bone reconstruction and Gazan hospitals lack the technology and medicine to do it.

At a political level, the peace process and binational solution have been dead for over a decade. Instead of discussing peace and diplomacy, Israeli Prime Minister Benjamin Netanyahu has defended something that he calls "economic peace," which is an approach to the conflict based on mutual economic cooperation. Jared Kushner, Trump's son-in-law and Middle East delegate, organized an "economic workshop" in June 2019 to entice investment in the Occupied Palestinian territories. Business leaders and finance ministers from all over the world came to a gathering in which political topics remained untouched. Palestinian officials were not consulted for the planning of the gathering and rejected attending meetings to discuss business in the region without discussing the illegal occupation and violation of human rights first. For Palestinians, any solution to the political conflict depends on ending the occupation, recognizing the national rights of the Palestinian people, and establishing an independent, sovereign, and viable State in the 1967 borders with Jerusalem as a shared capital.

The occupation of the West Bank and Gaza Strip has not only consolidated an apartheid system, but as I already mentioned, it serves as the prototype and laboratory of technologies of extermination, dispossession, and control of undesired populations for the rest of the world. Aside from being a leader in the production and sales of security and war technologies, Israel was the first country and Netanyahu the first president to use racist hate language and "self-truth" (or "alternative facts") in the public sphere and through social media, starting a new form of governing across the world in the twenty-first century. Netanyahu was Israel's prime minister between 1996 and 1999 and since 2009 (he won the elections in 2013 and 2015). He was against the Oslo Agreements in 1993 and during his first term as prime minister, he constantly violated the agreements made by the Israeli governments that preceded him and had committed to giving back the Palestinian territory to the 1967 borders. Netanyahu openly rejects the "two State solution" because he infringed on the accord known as the Roadmap. Signed in 2003, the Roadmap posited step-by-step the establishment of a Palestinian sovereign State coexisting next to Israel.[2] This agreement implied ending the violence generated by the Second Intifada, stopping the construction of settlements in the West Bank, lifting the siege in Gaza, reforming Palestinian institutions, accepting Israel's right to exist, and establishing a Palestinian sovereign state. The Roadmap, however, was never implemented and Netanyahu continued Ariel Sharon and Ehud Olmert's policies of settlement expansion across the West Bank. As we have seen, these policies are designed to intensify Palestinian suffering to the maximum to break them down.

In 2009, Netanyahu gave a speech famous for its controversial declarations at the Bar Ilan University. He proclaimed that Jerusalem was Israeli territory and that Palestinians had to recognize Israel as a Jewish State with an undivided Jerusalem as capital. This would imply obliterating the possibility of return for the Palestinian refugees (albeit symbolic), because the return of exiled and diaspora Palestinians precisely threatens Israel's existence as a State for the Jewish people only. Netanyahu also declared that it was not possible to stop the expansion of West Bank settlements due to "natural demographic growth" and migration of populations. It is said that with the speech, Netanyahu shut the door to any negotiation that could result in establishing something permanent with the Palestinians.

Aside from Netanyahu's inflammatory words at Bar Ilan—considered to have been a response to Obama's "Cairo Speech" in which he announced a new beginning between the Islamic world and the US based on mutual respect and understanding—Netanyahu has been repeatedly accused of crushing truth and inciting hatred through "alternative facts" in election campaigns, social media posts, and public declarations. "Alternative facts" (a term from Kellyanne Conway, Donald Trump's counselor) are a repertoire of preconceived ideas and lies that are very popular with the public and keep Netanyahu in newspapers' headlines. In an article from the *Guardian*, reporter Dahlia Scheindin explained how at every conjuncture of his mandates Netanyahu has coined a "trope" or figure that responds to specific political needs that he promotes aggressively to achieve popularity amongst his constituents (as Trump, López Obrador, and others do). For instance, in the context of the incident against the Turkish boat the Mavi Marvara, which was part of a larger flotilla travelling to Gaza in 2009 to symbolically break the Israeli siege, bringing activists and humanitarian aid to Gaza, he called any kind of criticism of the State of Israel and its policies "delegitimation."[3] Since then, however, it has become acceptable in Israel (and later on, in the rest of the world) to give openly racist speeches in the public sphere. For instance, that year, politician Avigdor Lieberman campaigned to attract Arab-Israeli voters and one of his sarcastic slogans was "Only Lieberman speaks Arabic." In Israel, latent racism became exchange currency in the public sphere and social media before anywhere else in the world in the twenty-first century, to the extreme that at the heart of the Knesset (the Israeli parliament), Naftali Benett, member of the Jewish Home party, allowed herself in 2012 to declare that the Arab members of parliament (and Arabs in general) are "savages."

For the past ten years more or less, millions of racist commentaries have been circulating in social media along with attacks against opinion columns in Israel. In 2015 Netanyahu made one of his most scandalous declarations to date: "Back then, Hitler refused to exterminate the Jews, he wanted to expel them. And Haj Amin al-Husseini (a nationalist and religious Palestinian leader under the British mandate) went to Hitler and said: 'If you expel them, they will all come here (to Palestine).'" According to Netanyahu, Hitler answered, "And what should I do with them?" "Burn them," supposedly answered the Mufti. When being confronted with the falsity of his declaration, Netanyahu responded, "I didn't want to absolve Hitler of his responsibility, but to show that the Father of the Palestinian Nation wanted to destroy the Jews even before the occupation existed."[4]

Netanyahu's brand of Zionist extremism is based on references to the Holocaust, pogroms, and historical anti-Semitism. In a 2006 discourse in the Knesset, as the war against Lebanon ended, he declared, "The truth is that if Israel deposed the weapons, there would be no more Israel. If Arabs deposed the weapons, there would be no more war." In 2018 he declared in Brazil, "Israel is not the State of all of its citizens. According to the Law we approved Israel as the Nation-State of the Jewish people—and none else's." In March 2019, he caused another scandal as he echoed Hitler, tweeting from the prime minister's official account that "the weak are massacred" and "the strong survive."[5] Many noted the parallel with similar declarations by Hitler in a speech in Munich in 1923 despising the weak. Another worrying declaration Netanyahu made was that he would "annihilate" the enemies of his country, a threat that he made standing next to an atomic reactor in August 2019.

In retrospect, Netanyahu was the prototype for a new form of government, practicing a form of political speech rooted in self-truth, racism, and hatred and destroying the public sphere and diplomacy. Donald Trump has used hatred speech and inflammatory declarations in social media just as Netanyahu has as a strategy to maintain his popularity. Trump, moreover, is an unreserved champion of the Israeli cause. At the beginning of his mandate in 2017 he changed the US's historical role of peace mediator between Israel and Palestine when he unilaterally moved the US embassy from Tel Aviv to Jerusalem. The meaning of this gesture is an explicit message to the Palestinians: Palestinian national reality and the rights of Palestinians do not exist. At that moment, which was at the beginning of his term, Trump cut diplomatic relations with Palestinian leadership and slashed a subsidy to the United Nations Agency for Palestinian Refugees in the Middle East (UNRWA), which had been 1.2 billion dollars a year, reducing it to a third of the original amount. He declared that if violations by Israeli perpetrators of human rights were judged in an international tribunal, the US would avenge them by freezing diplomatic relations and through sanctions, embargo, and annihilation. In June 2019 he shut down the Palestinian Liberation Organization's (PLO) office in Washington, DC, and recognized the illegal annexation by Israel of the Golan Heights, where one of the settlements is called Trump Heights. US support to Israel has always been unconditional, but never before had the United States served as an extension of the militarized Israeli border. In September 2019, a Palestinian student, Ismail Ajjawi, arrived in Boston to begin his studies as a medical student with a scholarship by Harvard University. Upon arrival to the US, he was interrogated by immigration officials who questioned his religious beliefs, examined his cell phone and computer, and pointed at postings by his friends in social media critiquing US policy. Ismail's visa was canceled and he was deported to Lebanon where his family lives, until the scandal his case generated put pressure on the US government and he was enabled to come back and begin classes at Harvard that fall. The new policies against Palestinians in Israel and elsewhere signified the end of diplomacy as we knew it in the twentieth century and the end of the historical role of the United States as peace mediator in the conflict.

Since Netanyahu and now Trump, the "Israeli Occupation" is no longer an occupation in terms of international humanitarian law. For the UN, a "military occupation" does not imply sovereignty of the occupier over the occupied nor the ability to transfer citizens from the occupied land and exert ethnic cleansing, property destruction, collective punishment, and settlement annexation. Israel's military occupation of the West Bank is thus revealed as one of the phases of Zionist colonization of historical Palestine, a process that began over a hundred years ago and that has been accelerated by Trump and Netanyahu. On the eve of Israeli elections and to quiet scandals around corruption cases against him, on September 10, 2019, Netanyahu declared that if voters returned him to power, he would annex the majority of the West Bank and the Jordan Valley. The implications would be a dramatic change in the form of the conflict, reducing the Palestinian state to an enclave surrounded by Israel; Trump has expressed being open to annexation.[6] The result of the 2019 election was inconclusive, and Netanyahu and his opponent in the elections, Benny Gantz, negotiated a coalition government from September to March 2020 while it was being debated in Israel whether Netanyahu would face trial for the various accusations against him for corruption, fraud, breach of faith, and other criminal charges. In March 2020, Benny Gantz opted to join Prime Minister Netanyahu in a new government, breaking with half of his party. Both agreed to rotate as prime minister, each serving for eighteen months. In the interim, Gantz would be foreign minister and deputy prime minister.

The most recent chapter in the story of the Israeli occupation of Palestine is the normalization of diplomatic and economic relations between Israel and the United Arab Emirates, a deal brokered by the United States upon Israeli agreement of "halting temporarily" plans to annex all of the occupied Palestinian territories in the West Bank. The Palestinian Authority rejected and denounced the trilateral deal and called in its ambassador in the UAE. This open public alliance between Israel and one of the most reactionary, antidemocratic monarchies in the world is another big blow for the Palestinians: the UAE is the first Arab country to officially recognize Israel, which means loss of support by an Arab government of the Palestinians, although Arab public opinion considers Israel to be a great danger and is not necessarily represented by monarchies like the UAE. Meanwhile, Israeli tanks and warplanes have been attacking Gaza for the past seven days (in the second week of August 2020), allegedly as retaliation for incendiary balloons launched by Hamas. The current situation for Palestinians is untenable, and they will keep on demanding equal national rights and self-determination.

If we discuss "Palestine today" in the Mexican context, it is key to understand that we are speaking not only of the Middle East, but about the rest of the world. As I already mentioned, Israel is the vanguard of the implementation of technologies of repression, control, and dispossession of redundant populations, the gradual destruction of the public sphere by means of self-truths and hate speech. We must consider that the bases of domination, colonial exploitation, and Western supremacy are not proper to Israel but are rooted in the Modern European State, a model of colonial occupation that has been exported to the rest of the world based on the accumulation of wealth through the exploitation of human labor, the displacement of millions of people who live off their lands, and the destruction of the commons (the extraction of "natural resources" or the "zonification" of territories). The logic at the basis of the Israeli-Palestinian conflict is the geopolitical and sociocultural basis of our own society, rooted in control and the privatization of land taken away from originary peoples for the purpose of accumulation administered by the Nation-State in the name of progress and development. The dispossession of land may take many forms, but it happens mainly through war with the purpose of destroying the will of the enemy and her capacity to resist by any means possible, but above all it happens by attacking citizens and their support and solidarity survival networks. The war being currently waged in Mexico is not a war between two clearly identified parties as enemies as is the Israeli-Palestinian conflict; the Neoliberal War in Mexico is perpetrated by ambiguous forces attacking the originary populations to dispossess them of their territories and destroy the commons. The tools used to cleanse the territories are forced disappearance, extortion, and terrorizing communities. In this context, to continue Felipe Calderón and Enrique Peña Nieto's project of militarizing the country makes no sense unless to give continuity to the neoliberal, colonialist extractivist project based on the control of space for dispossession and destruction.

The fact that the Palestinian ordeal reproduces itself throughout the world makes them exemplary in their resistance against occupation, aggressions, and Israeli dispossession. They resist giving in, being coopted. Right now, although their government collaborates with their oppressors, Palestinians keep on affirming their presence and ties to their land through the practice of *sumud* (perseverance, dignity), waiting to see what new form their struggle may take. And for the moment we can support their boycott campaign against Israel and hope for the possible advent of a Third Intifada.

Chimalistac Postcard

I'm introduced to her at a party where we both are guests; I fall deeply in love; I want to stick by her as much as possible (with polite distance). I visit her home, she appears with a journalist vest denoting her profession worn over a grey jogging suit and youthful sneakers. She receives me in a tiny living room with two elegant white couches adorned by half a dozen small yellow cushions, and by a big one embroidered with an endearing cartoon of the former future Leftist candidate to the presidency, hands and smile full of promises. The room is surrounded by bookshelves beautifully mounted before mirrors that light up the room. I timidly peek at the photos in the frames scattered around, look at the piles of magazines in the bathtub at the guest toilet, at the beautiful and narrow patio that only has space to lodge one planter with four rows of flower pots; they are all in bloom. I am not sure her health is one of her concerns, but I intuit fragility in her body, although it doesn't affect her energy for writing. She just happened to finish a manuscript of over five hundred pages, which will become a two-volume novel in which she returns to the country and history of her ancestors. She comes from a Mexico that is long gone. Through her, I yearn to get close and touch that Mexico. So I slip into her soft spoken words, while she in turn, seeks to meet me in my Mexico, also through my words. "And do your female students participate actively in class now?" An anecdote she shares is when she met Susan Sontag who had come to UNAM in the 1960s to discuss feminism. They recall that it seemed like she had only addressed the male students because during the discussion following her talk, their female peers remained timidly silent. "That has changed, Elenita, but they still hesitate, doubt themselves." I myself had a hard time being able to get my voice out without shaking and feeling panic about not being able to say intelligent things. I wish she'd let me listen to her talk for hours about her life, her family, her books. But like the fine journalist she is, she keeps putting the spotlight back on me. Growing confident, I tell her a bit about myself. I am in heaven with her attention, but after, when I think about it, I feel a bit foolish. Only the best journalists are able to fuse the interior and exterior of what or whom they have before them.

Together we lament the death of Francisco Toledo, an incommensurable loss. She introduces me to "Monsi" and "Váis" and I immediately read a cartography of affects, complicities, and resonances around her built in a Mexico where a community of friends contributed with courageous words and strong arguments and protests to put on the foundations for democracy in Mexico at the eve of the twenty-first century, after decades of battles.

She is a mirror or maybe a resonance chamber through which the amplitude of the world is embroidered as stories of the forgotten and the angels, architects, murdered students and prisoners, to whom she has lent her voice. Through her, I sense the echoes of unforgettable women like Lilus Kikus and Chiruelita, the indomitable, the little goats, the *soldaderas*, and the guerrilleras, the abortionists, the *juchitanas*. She has drawn them for us to anchor our imaginary genealogies and sororities. She talks as she writes, with a Spanish from before, full of charming expressions and words from yesteryear mixing impudence and quiet outrageousness with humility, elegance, and witty charm. I feel the need to try to step up and carry on her legacy, reconfigured by the challenges of the present. Thank you E, for so much!

Uprooting, Rights, and State Violence

It is possible that the epidemic of narcissism and the illusion of self-sufficiency are tied to modern uprooting, which we could think of as a different way to conceptualize what Marxist thinkers defined as "alienation." Uprooting is the condition of not feeling part of a whole, of a collective destiny. According to Venezuelan writer Carlos Rangel, uprooting is a condition inherited from colonialism.[1] That is why an alternative to the impasses of the present would be to find ways of creating epistemologies that could help prevent uprooting starting from that acknowledgment of the interconnection of interdependency amongst everyone and everything. And to think of rooting up as a basic need of the soul that, for the moment, we have no way of fulfilling. Another paradox emerges here: if we are the descendants of European colonizers and root ourselves consciously, Where and what happens to originary peoples undergoing constant threat of displacement and uprooting? Cristina Rivera Garza's *La autobiografía del algodón* (2020; Autobiography of cotton) is a search for roots and belonging departing from displacement. For Cristina, belonging is built by inhabiting, and inhabiting means the Jungian idea of wholeness: "inhabiting the quaternity—land, sky, divinity, community."[2] It is also looking after the quaternity. Her *autobiografía del algodón* is an extraordinary text, embroidered with different textures: travel chronicle, novel, historical archive, and literary analysis leading to a search for the authors' roots. She tells the stories of her grandparents, parents, and extended family traversed by dreams of modernity, development, and the Mexican revolution. Originally miners, her grandparents flourished producing cotton financed by Lázaro Cárdenas' government. In the 1930s, after a cotton-workers' strike in Estación Camarón in the northern state of Nuevo León, famously documented by José Revueltas, the government began to distribute land to new settlers. Each family got fifteen hectares with a credit from the Banco de Crédito Ejidatal. This social experiment saw the birth of a rural middle class inhabiting cities designed by engineers. When the cotton agroindustry ran its course after having drained the soil, the population moved to urban regions. Rivera Garza attests to the fact that the trace left by cotton is inhabited in the present by violence and illness. Her trip across the places where her ancestors lived make her notice that we are guests in the world and that we share it, and that our link to the earth is made up of ties to our environment and to others. The traces that are there and that precede us are "traces that embrace and alter us, that force us to recognize the plural root of our steps." She also notes that we are usurpers as much as guests to these traces, because the place we inhabit was once occupied by someone else: "the displacement of whom makes it possible for me to be here? What eviction or what flight opened up the terrain I stand on?"[3]

For French philosopher Simone Weil, the condition of being rooted is the most important and the least recognized need of humans. According to Weil, uprootedness is contagious because it propagates and suppresses local life, it creates living death, which is the most dangerous illness human societies can be exposed to.[4] How did we come to exist in societies suffering from uprooting (alienation)? According to Weil, when the State was constituted, it channeled and benefited from the collective need of "national" unity. The cost of national sovereignty, however, was the loss of the past and tradition and the destruction of the communal sphere. From there, States bled communities within their territories of their moral essence. Once they were no longer able to extract nourishment from their territories, the Nation-States generated lethargy in their citizens while public institutions began to generate disdain, rejection, and mocking. The State of an uprooted people is for Weil naturally an object of hatred, disgust, mockery, and fear, even though as an absolute value, the "Fatherland" demands complete loyalty and abnegation, supreme sacrifice. At the same time, the State systemically exercises violence against the population.

In the early 1980s, Elena Poniatowska wrote *Fuerte es el silencio* (Strong is the silence), a book where she speaks of two Mexicos: a civil one and a militarized one of clandestine jails and mass graves. Today we can add a third: that of a permanent state of exception, for which the State delegated violence to paramilitaries and criminals.

If we knew our own history, the number of disappeared and mass graves in 2020 should not surprise us. Elenita recounts that in 1978, Herberto Castillo, leader of the Partido Mexicano de Trabajadores (Mexican Workers Party), declared that there were hundreds of military clandestine jails full of people kidnapped by the White Brigade and accused of "political crimes"; in the Campo Militar there were 150 illegal detainees who were also tortured under the pretext that they "conspired against the government."[5] During the communist prosecution of the Dirty War, thousands of people disappeared after being apprehended by the authorities: in some cases their bodies were found mutilated or in police establishments where they appeared to have committed suicide. Since then, it has been common for public power to practice extralegal detentions (or kidnap people) through paramilitary bodies acting at the margins of or covered up by the government. There also existed groups of mothers looking for their disappeared children and claiming justice. In her book, Poniatowska suggests calling the disappeared "kidnapped" because when a person is "disappeared," she is gone without a trace, no one hears from him or her ever again. But in truth, these people were kidnapped because their kidnappers know their whereabouts but will not disclose them.

Forty years after the Dirty War, kidnappings by military and paramilitary organisms are the order of the day across the country. As I already mentioned, Dawn Marie Paley argues that what we call the War against Drugs is a continuation of State violence through government, paramilitary, and criminal groups that continue the practice of kidnapping campesinos, migrants, students, deported people, community leaders, or others in resistance against dispossession of their lands or the destruction of the commons.[6] For Dawn, this war is directed against the popular-communitarian sector behind which are extermination and land devastation campaigns perpetrated or supervised by the State. The disappeared are labeled as cartels and indeed, cartels and paramilitaries play a key role in echoing State violence against the people. In the official discourse, however, criminals are prosecuted and the innocent are collateral damage. But in truth, the redundant populations are being treated as insurgents through an apparatus conceptualized by Paley as "expanded counterinsurgency." This apparatus encompasses multiple and apparently disconnected violent events throughout Mexico characterized by 1) confusion of the perpetrators in a narrative of a conflict based on "narcos"; 2) the amplification of the category of the insurgent; and 3) the use of a complex of violences that ranges from spectacular death to massive forced disappearance.

What results from the social terror propagated by this "Neoliberal War" (a continuation of the Dirty War) is social discipline that serves the system by delivering a message for communities and groups, but also attempts to subject the work force and keep it in check and adequate in size according to the market's needs. What Paley describes as "expanded counterinsurgency" indeed represents a continuation of the 1960s and 1970s Dirty War against communist youth and campesinos across the country. In the 1960s, State violence concentrated in Guerrero, the poorest state of the country, against mostly a rural population. The official discourse justified repression in Guerrero as a response to a criminal threat. In 1971, Hermenegildo Cuenca Díaz, State defense secretary, launched the Plan Telaraña, a mission to eradicate the guerrilla insurgents who were criminalized, prosecuted, captured, tortured, murdered, and disappeared. Back then, prisoners were buried alive or thrown into the sea from helicopters. Illegal detentions and interrogations, transportation to military installations that worked as clandestine jails, and executions were the order of the day. We speak about systemic genocide in the state of Guerrero alone between 1973 and 1978, along with the destruction of entire villages in the Atoyac Sierra. Back then, disappearance was a form of counterinsurgency and a weapon of terror by the State.

For its part, disappearance under the current Neoliberal War is one of the elements of the expanded counterinsurgency apparatus that appears in most cases as a "crime by armed groups" against youth, poor men, and migrants. As a Dirty War counterinsurgency tactic, neoliberal disappearance is deliberately traumatic and visible to demobilize political popular resistance. As Paley observes, many of the same tactics of the Dirty War are being used in the so-called War against Drugs, which is now serving the purpose of exercising control over the victims and their communities, fracturing social networks, and spreading terror. Patterns of contemporary disappearances occur in zones where economic interests could be benefited by dispossession of local inhabitants, as contemporary disappearance has as its main goal social and territorial control through terror, hindering the people's capacity to weave alliances.

Women and young children are also victims in this war, especially women. Disappearance or kidnapping of loved ones breaks people from within, as well as families and eventually communities. Forms of life and the possibilities of making a living are constantly under threat because the State, no matter the party or regime, is now in charge of administering (sometimes through omission) the machine of the distribution of death of redundant populations.

The redundant populations are described by Elenita in *Fuerte es el silencio* as "angels." They were uprooted people seeking to make a living in the big city. Today the angels are the hundreds of thousands of people forced to migrate, fleeing hunger and violence in the places where they are from.

The immense flux of people at the global scale could seemingly shatter the ideological apparatus of Nation-States, which have responded to mass migration with deportation, repression, expulsion, detention, separation. In this context, we can think of the Migrant Caravan (which travels in the opposite sense from the deportees) as an exercise of transnational civil disobedience in which men, women, children travel together to accompany and protect themselves, risking crossing the border to the US and reuniting with their families, looking for a better life before Donald Trump could fulfill his threat to shut the borders (which was enacted as a measure to contain the COVID-19 pandemic). The migrant exodus had also been a form of civil resistance against the conditions in which redundant populations are forced to survive in their places of origin. They decide to make the trip and risk their lives, fleeing violence and hunger. They uproot not with the purpose of earning a salary and modernizing (as in the 1960s and 1970s), but as a means of warding off the danger of death where they live as noncitizens, of seeking security, inclusion, education, and labor: the basic needs of the soul according to Simone Weil. Redundant populations, however, emit sounds that can't be recognized by the neoliberal State because they do not conform to the neoliberal lexicon of political demands. Although they are basic demands, they lack legibility because they exist on the exploited side of the injurious forms of dependency we inherited from colonialism: they are the prey needed by the capitalist society to keep on going. If the basis of all society is interdependence, with colonialism interdependence becomes depredation, and thus relationships based on injury and exploitation, on the mercantilization and exploitation of bodies and nature are established. That is why the exploited are not recognized as capable of enunciating political demands; their voices move through noise and language, registering their unacceptable condition as excluded at the level of the body, bodies living at the limit, living with irresoluble sorrows and political suffering.

The Nation-State supposedly guarantees citizens basic rights to cover the soul's needs. The problem is that this abstract entity lacks the capacity to generate obligations among the people that could give way to guaranteeing rights for everyone. The Nation-State governs by administering the rights of the citizens and the situation of a permanent state of exception of others. The first step to solve this impasse would be to dispossess the State from its status as guarantor of the vital needs of the soul, of "human rights," recognizing that the colonial heritage that structures our society is predatory, running on an unstoppable machinery of death.

COVID-19

In his classic text "The Theater and the Plague" (1938), Antonin Artaud described the plague as a situation in which "life succumbs." During the plague pandemic, life is disjointed from culture, and before we can even discuss culture, we must consider that the world is starving, and that culture never saved man from the preoccupation of living better or from being hungry. In further discussing the relationship between life and culture, Artaud argues that in order to live we must be able to satisfy bodily needs, but we also need to believe in that which makes us live: thought systems. Although foreign to our bodies, thought systems are either within us or we live within them, so even if we may think of life and culture separately, culture rules our most subtle acts and decisions because culture is the spirit present in things. Indeed culture does not feed us, but it definitely drives our decisions toward finding ways of sustaining ourselves; culture is also vital for humanity because we think through systems of forms, signs, and representations, all of which give meaning to our lives. For Artaud, however, during the plague pandemic both life and poetry slip away. Social forms, order, morality all disintegrate and collapse, all while psychological disaster spreads. Artaud proceeds to provide a description of the plague's effects on the body: torn and collapsing tissue, organs growing heavy and turning to carbon, an unpleasant smell. These traits serve as a metaphor for the ravages undergone by the social body at large.

Differently from the plague, COVID-19 has not meant the collapse of social and civil order. On the contrary, during the most intense weeks of lockdown, streets were being kept, surveillance was enhanced, and everyone went through great efforts to continue living life as our hyperproductive normal. What became evident right away was not the fragility of life, but the fragility of the economy and the fact that every social relation passes through the market. In Mexico moreover, the problem is not so much contagion but deaths (with a death rate of over 12 percent) and the collapse of the economy.

A COVID-19 death is due to massive organ collapse caused by inflammation, analogous to the worldwide collapse of the economy and the destruction by fire of entire ecosystems . A COVID-19 patient dies from asphyxia, and being unable to breathe is a symptom of the pandemics of anxiety and panic humanity has been undergoing for the past couple of decades as labor has become more and more precarious, the productive market more demanding. COVID-19's watery lungs can also remind us of melting ice caps, and while the corpse of a Coronavirus victim shows no lesions, inner surfaces are intact except for overall inflammation due to cascading organ failure (encephalopathy, myocardial injury, hearth failure, coagulation dysfunction, and acute kidney injury) triggered by acute respiratory distress syndrome. The virus creates a barrier for oxygen, impeding its travel to the bloodstream, like the lowering levels of oxygen on earth due to deforestation and pollution.

Following Artaud, from the peculiarities, conditions, symptoms, and mysteries of the illness, we can construct the spiritual physiognomy of a disease that progressively chokes the body, as market-based human relationships are choking our (by now increasingly limited) capacity to sustain ourselves. Where is monetary exchange occurring? Who working in what is still making how much money? On what are we choosing to spend our money? Unlike with the plague, for which pyres were lit at random in public spaces to burn the dead, COVID-19 deaths are only visible in the interminable lines of people waiting to enter cemeteries or funeral homes to collect the incinerated remains of their beloved ones. If the plague was correlative to a powerful state of physical and social disorganization, COVID-19 is the powerful state of slowly choking the body along with our capacities to reproduce life collectively through markets. If the plague was seen by Artaud as undrained abscesses and thus the opportunity to drain moral and social abscesses, the COVID-19 virus cancels the body's capacity to keep itself alive with oxygen. Like the planet and the species it is home to, COVID-19 patients breathe for their lives. The virus means asphyxia of life on earth in progressive waves, reaching the most vulnerable populations and ecosystems first. Breathing and speaking also mean that the virus is spreading exponentially an invisible and lethal enemy: now every individual is a threat to society.

The world is killing itself unaware, starting with the fact that science and culture have become too expensive and thus are expendable for State capital-

FIGURE 14. Dana Schutz, *Floating Pieta* (2020). Signed and dated verso, oil on canvas, 223.5 × 223.5 cm. / 88 × 88 in. © Dana Schutz. Courtesy of the artist, Thomas Dane Gallery and David Zwirner Gallery. Photo: Jason Mandella

ism: the reign of technology begins as now the world is deprived of science and humanism. The virus expands through poor and precarious environments, bringing class and race issues immediately to the fore. COVID-19 is perceived as the presence of something that is foreign, anonymous, invisible, expansive, and lethal that will not go away. The virus is confronting us with the reality of death and mortality, which are anathema to our contemporary culture which is prone to prolonging illness to postpone death at any cost, where preventive medicine is just not profitable. Someone recently wrote that viruses are traces found on the crime scene. This virus survives in the cadaver whose life it has taken away.

To Dismantle the Engine

The title of a recent piece by Arundhati Roy is a harrowing: "Our Task Is to Disable the Engine."[1] As much as I agree with her, I wouldn't know where to start even to describe, let alone to think about how to dismantle "the engine." The more and more I think about it, everything appears to be so profoundly interlinked and tied to the logic of the market it's overwhelming. What is more, all upon which contemporary human subsistence is grounded (or "the engine") is fucked up: what we eat and how we produce and distribute food, healthcare and big pharma interests, environmental and human toxicity, extractivism and populist left-wing governments, privilege and redundant populations, the reproduction of life and the epidemics of anxiety and depression, how we consume and generate energy, how we produce, communicate, and share meaning. So when I think that our task is to "dismantle the engine," I think about the fact that Ecuador's development has been led by Chinese investment and that to repay its debt, the country has given China 3 million of its 8.1 million hectares of Amazon rainforest to exploit oil fields.[2] Or how in India the government gave permission in the spring of 2020 to convert large quantities of harvested rice into ethanol to make hand sanitizer and fuel while people in India began to fall ill and starve.[3] The harrowing enormity of the task to "dismantle the engine" might reside in the fact that "the engine" itself is not only what grounds a portion of humanity's subsistence on earth, but also what gives meaning to modern human existence. Because how else would we even conceive fossil fuel extraction, given the devastation it causes? And how is it possible that we let people to starve? Is "the engine" the market, grounded on the denigration of life, outside of which we are at the moment incapable of surviving? What is behind the possibility of conceiving of denigrating life to guarantee the subsistence of a few in the first place?

So allow me to stumble as I try to articulate this. With modernity, man as opposed to god became the source of reason to overcome the chaos of the universe. The radical secularization of humankind put man and eventually, the individual, at the center of everything. The meaning of human life on earth became humanity's struggle against death, decay, entropy: specifically, the dark matters of nature. Human effort came to be geared at enhancing human beings through technology and science to expand life, to make it more comfortable, to eradicate disease, to achieve transcendence without god, to alleviate the tasks to make it easier to reproduce and sustain life. Transcendence has been sought symbolically through art, but it was also accomplished via space travel, which solved the riddle of the ontological discontinuity between above and below. It became evident though, that transcendence via space travel is limited; it is rather a reminder that the Earth will remain forever a finite monad and that humans, even as they are emancipated from the Earth, will always need the inclusion of an environment to sustain life and assure vital functions. This brings to mind Claire Denis's film *High Life* (2017), which I consider to be a feminist take on the sci-fi genre of space travel films in which bodily needs or reproduction are never an issue. A group of criminals (Who else would volunteer to travel on a mission toward a black hole?) facing either life imprisonment or the death penalty have accepted this suicide mission as a form of redemption. All the passengers are young adults except Dr. Dibs (Juliette Binoche), who looks after their health, well-being, and order inside the spacecraft (designed by Olafur Eliasson). Dibs (a convict also, for murdering her husband and children) is obsessed with reproduction. A "fuck box" is one of the features on board, to alleviate the prohibition against having sex, so Dibs collects semen from the box to implant it in the women hoping to make a baby in space. One of the passengers indeed becomes pregnant, but through a series of conflicts that unfold between the crewmembers, everyone dies except Willow, the baby bred by Dibs, and her father Monte. In the film, scenes of fatherhood and the daily tasks needed to reproduce life and survive are interlinked with images that dwell on the physicality of bodily fluids and care and carnal existence. If the imaginary of transcendence via space travel means detachment from human biological needs and functions (premised by the philosophical abstraction of consciousness from the body), Claire Denis's film confirms that in spite of humankinds' scientific and technological achievements, humans will always be dependent on the environment to survive.

The human dream of secular immortality, fighting entropy through technology and science, moreover, has had dystopian manifestations in transhumanism, cryonics, rejuvenation, and Silicon Valley's ideology to download our brain into machines. In this imaginary, it is not only that eugenics and social Darwinism have served to justify who gets left out from bodily transcendence, but the socio-political and environmental costs of the modernist fight against death and decay through technology and science have been invisibilized. This is one of the premises of DeLillo's *Zero K* (2016), a vision of a future world where Westerners like Jeff and Ross can be members of a cult to eliminate death. Jeff travels to a hospice to say farewell to his stepmother, an archeologist who is dying of several diseases. The hospice is Convergence, a cryonic suspension facility where the dead are frozen in anticipation of the day when resuscitation is medically feasible. Ross is Jeff's father and one of the main investors and advocates of the Convergence project. Jeff is a skeptic and opposing his father, remains rooted in the real world, a world that is ridden with natural and political disasters, in which the possibility of eternal life not only remains uncertain, but is an instrument of power and only for a few, whose life comes to be sustained solely through the technosphere.

The technosphere is the material expression of the simplification or reduction of reproductive and life-functions to overcome biological barriers and entropy through technology. The technosphere, in other words, is a supplement humans have created to help overcome the limits of "human nature" in so far as humans cannot self-energize or self-reproduce. In that regard, the technosphere has allowed us to accomplish or increase production and reproduction with less human effort. The technosphere, moreover, is the main tool humans have to fight decay, entropy, and death, and it comprises all the structures humans have built to keep them alive on the planet: houses, factories, farms, computer systems, smartphones, CDs, waste in landfills, spoil heaps but also mines, roads, airports, shipping ports, computer systems. The mass of the technosphere amounts to 50 kilos for every square meter on Earth's surface, a total of 30 trillion tons that coexist with the diminishing hydrosphere (water, cryosphere, frozen polar regions) and the biosphere (all of Earth's living organisms). The cost of the technosphere is global warming, environmental devastation, and the decimation of the biosphere and hydrosphere. This is because, like humans, the technosphere needs external energy input, which is not sustainable as long as it comes from fossil fuels that will eventually deplete. The external energization of both the technosphere and of humans is currently subject to market forces and this is how the engine exists as an essential market relationship.

The human "miracle," moreover, has been achieved at a heavy cost: deforestation, soil erosion, water depletion, pollution, mass extinction, slavery, and diet-related diseases are just some of the side effects of the technosphere and its dependence on the market to function. In addition, the benefits of the technosphere are not distributed equally among humanity. The consequence is that the human body has become a geopolitical drama because public health infrastructure has been devastated in the past thirty years and is not enough to assure everyone's well-being. Pharmaceutical corporate interests have become class interests, exacerbated by the current COVID-19 pandemic crisis.

The modernist ideals behind human-led transcendence manifest today in the "engine" in which healthcare, communication, the food that we eat, the energy we consume all pass through the market and are interlinked. Take almonds for instance, a popular nut and milk that is consumed all over the world. Eighty percent of the almonds consumed globally come from California's Central Valley.[4] Although the Valley is drought stricken, almond fields are expanding because they are making corporations (not small farmers) rich. Technically a desert, the California almond fields rely on irrigation water guided from mountain ranges in the north and east. The Valley has been hit by drought in the past few years, but because the almond fields are making corporate farmers rich, the fields are nonetheless growing. Bear in mind that a whole gallon of water is needed to produce a single almond, and in order to keep production going, farmers are tapping underground water. Experts worry that the combination of over pumping and drought could be catastrophic for the Central Valley, whose economy depends on being one of the world's most productive farming areas.[5] Across the Valley, moreover, the water pumping frenzy is causing severe strains: villagers have seen their wells dry up, there is arsenic in tap water, people even need to survive on bottled water provided by the county. As underground water depletes, the remaining water picks up higher concentration of minerals from deep in the earth, and when the orchards are watered with this hard water, salts build up in the soil and will eventually poison the soil and the trees. This situation in the Central Valley became the subject of journalistic investigation in 2015 and has gotten much worse since. As Huiying Ng argues, when earth's metabolic rhythms are made to converge with anthropocentric needs—as they have since modernity; humanity is at the center of everything—the nutrient cycling process is disrupted, leading to environmental catastrophe.[6] The drama behind the globalized production of almonds is illustrative of how our entire food system is based on industrial farming as a way to cheapen and mass-produce foods. This means that to sustain ourselves we are devaluing life, killing ourselves and our planet. But there is no such thing as cheap food. Food is the substance that ties us directly to the world's living (and dying) ecosystems as well as to one another: perhaps if we start by being able to value food properly, we could transform our lives, landscapes, and societies.

Humans, moreover, not only need to be connected to a natural sphere that permanently assures their vital functions. We are members of a symbolic species and require a cultural sphere in which to thrive. It is known that Western modernity is premised on a march to progress (or human emancipation from its ties to earth) through technology breaking away from tradition to announce the future or the new. In order to compensate for the loss of tradition, modernity invented ideological or historical grand narratives and implemented memorializing mechanisms. If the elimination of the past includes the destruction of humanity's sacred link to the world as I mentioned earlier, the meaning of human existence on earth is humanity's individualized transcendence. The meaning of life on earth, however, has become increasingly an abstraction, transforming all that signifies (language, symbols) into communication without community, abstract and thus easily manipulable. I can't help but to think of the *palabrero* in Ciro Guerra and Cristina Gallego's *Birds of Passage* (2018), a character or figure that functions as the medium/negotiator between two communities in dispute. Once the *palabrero* is murdered, everything goes to hell. In the film, the murder of the carrier of meaning is the ultimate transgression that brings doom for all, highlighting the role of language and the production of meaning in sustaining communities. In addition, modernity/modernization has seen the gradual disappearance of rituals or symbolic actions that generate community. With the digitalization of communication, we are interconnected but without true closeness. Digital communication reinforces the place of the human ego at the center (we are invited to communicate our opinions, needs, and desires) while isolation and loneliness increase. Social reproduction has also migrated to digital media, especially now in the COVID-19 crisis it has completely replaced physical closeness. As tech companies are seeking to profit from isolation as a laboratory for a permanent and highly profitable no-touch future, all community experience is being lost. A future in which our homes are never again exclusively personal space but also our schools, doctors' offices, gyms, and jail is premised on the integration of technology into every aspect of civic life, what Naomi Klein recently called "The Screen New Deal."[7]

In these COVID-19 times, not only technology companies (whose earnings exponentially increased with the lockdown), but the health industry is seeking a potential bonanza. The market is flooded with garbage anti-body tests for the virus; although the vaccine is still a year away, everyone knows that big pharma companies are lobbying everywhere for certain State positions to allow for monopolies to distribute the medicine, which is antithetical to public interest. These phenomena are all reminders of how our culture, our world is grounded on the denigration of life, under-scored by the pressure to reopen the economy too soon and to have to face the dilemma of either going to work and putting food on the table while being vulnerable to COVID-19 or starving. The "engine" itself is a threat to human survival: it can't guarantee food security for humanity or create jobs or guarantee people's income or a meaningful social role. The majority of the global population's lives are currently not only unmournable, but unworthy of being lived.

Instead of protecting humans, the objective of the COVID-19 crisis poli-cies in the US is to protect the markets as is the case in Mexico: the govern-ment is allowing unemployment to skyrocket, and small and medium busi-nesses (PyMES) are racing toward bankruptcy because the government hasn't called either for the national suspension of rent nor for paid sick leave, nor has it even given tax breaks. This under the ideological prem-ise of not bailing out the private sector and leaving a significant portion to its own devices (there are companies favored by the current regime). The country's Leftist government is paradoxically working for capitalism: once the pandemic is over, it will be private equity firms or narcos who will have the capacity to bail out the broken businesses through cheap debt. The government is also working for capitalism by taking shock-doctrine-style regressive measures, like the agreement signed April 29, 2020 to bring to a halt renewable energy production by transnational countries in Mexico, in which the SENER (Secretary of Energy) agreed to privilege fossil fuel energies and to make it difficult for transnational companies to connect and transmit energy through the CFE (Federal Electricity Commission) energy network. In 2013, an energy reform was approved in Mexico, enabling the participation of the private sector in electricity to produce solar and aeolic energy.[8] Overall, renewable energies were welcomed as a step forward, but the way the corporations "entered" communities across the country violated people's rights: the corporations paid a minimum to rent lands to exploit them, they failed to do consultation forums with the owners, and in many cases the contracts were straightforwardly abusive because no sanctions were stipulated if companies failed to pay *ejidatarios* rent for their lands or if ecosystems were destroyed. Thus in Mexico, clean energy (represented by the presence of at least 154 companies with permission to generate electricity with renewable energy) came with the cost of violating human rights in the states of Oaxaca, Veracruz, Nayarit, Guerrero, Jalisco, Puebla, Nuevo León, Baja California, Guanajuato, Tamaulipas, Aguascalientes, San Luis Potosí, Mexico State, Baja California Sur, Sinaloa, Sonora, Chiapas, Coahuila, Durango, Yucatán, Chihuahua, Zacatecas, Michoacán, and Querétaro.

It obvious that the fight for renewable energy goes hand in hand with a struggle to protect the people affected by the implementation of such infrastructure and their lands. Clearly, the problem with the agreement recently signed by the SENER, is that the Mexican president has now officially joined the ranks of climate change deniers who are also country leaders. As the CFE is mandated to privilege fossil fuel energy, the environmental cost goes without saying. Energy will also become more expensive for consumers. The Central Thermoelectric plant in Tula, Veracruz, will revert to being the main source of impact on air quality and public health. The plant operates with the dirtiest fuel, fuel oil, and it is said that the government is seeking to expand the practice of the burning of oil fuels.[9] The problem is a structural one: how to deprivatize (or reverse the neoliberal policy behind) the production of energy in Mexico and restitute the rights of the communities that have been violated by renewable energy? What we are getting is a regressive solution based on ideological principles at a heavy environmental and social cost.

The current Mexican government's ideological discourse is to "put the poor first." "The poor" is a vague category that includes the redundant populations, the working class, precarious workers, people living in sacrifice zones, farmers, campesinos and originary populations. The government claims that its policies are geared at solving the gap of inequality in the Mexican population and at distributing wealth more equally to alleviate poverty as scarcity. A document that circulated in May 2020 titled "La nueva normalidad" (The new normality) is a collective demand to stop megaprojects, addressed to the Mexican president and to governors of the states of Oaxaca, Chiapas, Yucatán, Quintana Roo, Campeche, Puebla, Morelos, and Veracruz. The public letter demands a stop to promoting an extractivist development model, and specifically, to canceling the construction of infrastructure for megaprojects like the Canal Interocéanico and the Mayan Train and to ending all mining activity in originary peoples' territories. In the document, the signatories (or "the poor") reject the militarization of their territories "to guard extractivist capital" or to repress them, and demand respect for the rights of originary peoples.[10] Once the quarantine ends, we need to run to stand alongside people defending their territories, in order to create a Mexican Standing Rock in Yucatán and elsewhere, massively mobilizing to join and support these demands.

It is clear, moreover, that the government's policies are aligned with protecting capital rather than humans and the environment, in line with the current mutation of neoliberal capitalism. The new system has been called "extractivism" or "primitive accumulation" (though we know it is around five hundred years old), but in a very convincing article, Jodi Dean describes how the current system is mutating toward "neofeudalism." Dean explains that the new social order is characterized by extreme inequality and mass serfdom in which the ones at the top have significantly more than the ones at the bottom and everyone is interlinked by feudal relations. Feudalism is characterized by a fundamental inequality that enables the direct exploitation of peasants by lords. The lord is not only both the manager and master of the process of production, but the lord also owns the entire process of social life. A new regime (which could describe the Mexican economic panorama: the State as the energy lord or the tax lord or the culture lord) in which a property-less underclass survives by servicing the needs of high earners as personal assistants, trainers, child-minders, cooks, cleaners. Under the neofeudal regime, the State is subjected to the market and accumulation occurs more than commodity production, through rent, debt, and privatization (of energy, railroads, broadband) and sovereignty over natural resources. The grounds for this new regime were prepared by the neoliberal strategy of undermining the authority of the Nation-State over its economy in the interest of advancing global trade. In the new schema, Nation-States promote and protect specific private corporations (the list of President Andrés Manuel López Obrador's cronies is well-known), and political power comes to be exercised as economic power applying not only taxes but also fines, asset seizures, licenses, patents, jurisdiction, and borders. In this system, technology acquires a key role as a source for extractivism: its owners are billionaires thanks to the cheap labor of their workers, the numbers of their users, and their tax breaks. Companies like Apple, Facebook, Microsoft, Amazon, and Alphabet come to behave as sovereign states themselves as their impact is now greater than Nation-States.[11]

One of the effects of feudalism is the loss of the capacity to reproduce the basic conditions of survival. . . . This is far from a vision anchored on the emancipation of "the poor" or "the working class" or "the originary populations" through megaprojects, by policies that incorporate redundant populations into the market as consumers, debtors, and cheap labor. According to Jodi Dean, capitalist relations of production and exploitation will continue under neofeudalism; vast fortunes will be amassed at the cost of extreme inequality and the destruction of life and the Earth that sustains it. The task is indeed to dismantle the engine.

The New Normality

We are living in the bright orange "new normality," a color and a name that have been given to the current stage of the COVID-19 epidemic. At the peak of the pandemic, "economic reactivation" is the first step being taken toward reopening social and educational activities in the country. So now sweatshops (I don't think the automobile industry ever shut down for fear of breaking off production chains between China, Mexico, and the US), construction, public places, transportation, and essential shops (but not restaurants) are being reactivated, everyone always keeping six feet apart and wearing facemasks. I have to note that doctors and mathematicians don't seem to quite agree on whether the curve has been flattened or not, if there ever was a contagion curve, if we have reached a peak that will intensify exponentially, the first wave of the pandemic not even being over. None knows for sure, and at this point, Mexico could be the country with the greatest mortality rate. The new normality has been implemented as a measure to alleviate the critical economic situation of thousands of people who are not working. They are facing a horrid dilemma (like in the US): to go out to work and risk contagion or to stay at home and starve along with their families. When we are facing the worst unemployment crisis in history, fear of the risk of hospital saturation has for sure been overcome.

The new normality also means that cultural, academic, archeological, and scientific research, along with environmental protection by State institutions, have been defunded while backward energy and economic development agendas based on fossil fuel extraction and combustion are being furthered. The budget cuts are so deep that I can almost see the ancien régime's agents of neoliberalization quietly chuckling to themselves. Three institutions have been welded together for the sake of saving taxpayer money: the Telecommunications Federal Institute (IFT), the Federal Commission of Economic Competition (Cofece), and the Energy Regulation Commission have been turned into the National Institute for Markets and Competition for Well-Being (INMECOB). Observers see this dismantling of democratic institutions as an excuse to replace them with bureaucracies more akin to the sensibility and interests of the current government.

In our new normality, we also imported the polarization—without the expressions of racial tension or the politicized wave of protests across the US—of the George Floyd murder by the Minneapolis police. (I wonder if the Mexican equivalent of Black Lives Matter could be Indigenous and Mestizo Lives Matter?) This polarization manifested shortly after the Floyd murder in Guadalajara, when mason Giovanni López Ramírez was killed by police for not wearing a facemask in public space. The murder provoked violent riots against Enrique Alfaro, the mayor of the city of Guadalajara. It must be noted that Alfaro's public measures regarding the COVID-19 pandemic not only have been progressive and admirable but have openly defied the federal government's policies. Early on, Guadalajara provided private transportation for doctors and nurses to their workplaces and established a "radar" to detect coronavirus cases; Alfaro has been wearing a facemask in public addresses and he suspended a tour of the State in response to the pandemic—the president has been doing the opposite. After the Guadalajara riots (in which police responded with violence and after Alfaro excused himself), in Mexico City, at the affluent Polanco neighborhood, a protest against the police murder of Giovanni López also took place in front of the "Jalisco House." During the protest, a group of masked demonstrators began to throw rocks, break glasses, and loot businesses on Reforma; after the demonstrations, graffiti sprayed throughout Polanco read, "Shut up white," "Are you watching hunger from your balcony?," "Shit white," and so on. That same week, during his daily morning address, the president presented a document of unknown origin that he said had been leaked to the president's office titled "Let's Rescue Mexico: BOA Project." According to the president, the document outlined a plan to discredit the government and to impoverish him, a plan that had been devised by the Bloque Opositor Amplio (BOA), composed of businessmen, politicians, and mass media figures. This evidently polarized further the public sphere with yet another shit storm.

In this context of overall fuckedupness, it must be noted that in Mexico class and race polarization have been historically apolitical, and that these two recent events have generated confusion and fueled hatred but without creating real debate about racism in Mexico. Worst of all, people are shocked and angry, threatened and emboldened but without addressing the blatant *blanquitud* behind the government's development program. Indeed, Mexico is racist; the nation's unconscious is ripe with self-hatred: Bárbara del Regil, an actor/influencer who posts a daily vigorexic exercise routine on Instagram Live alongside her teenage daughter, recently gave voice to this pervasive, unconscious *blanquitud*: while preparing to start her live workout routine, she approached her cell phone to modify the Instagram filter only to dismiss it out loud for making her skin look darker: "¡Ay qué prieta, no! ¡Qué feo!" ("Oh, no, I'm too dark! How ugly!")

Shit storms are succeeding each other at amazing speed, keeping citizens captive, shocked, outraged, and also entertained. Without hesitating I affirm that the Mexican president is getting worse than Trump: he's more outrageous, vulgar, undiplomatic, and schizophrenic, more of a liar, a misogynist, self-entitled, populist. Closer to Bibi Netanyahu, maybe. López Obrador points fingers at "the rich," demonizes the private sector (his main ally in the megaprojects) and neoliberalism, and endlessly repeats generic phrases against corruption, diatribes against his adversaries, religious rants. His *Mañanera* or Daily Morning Address is the equivalent of Trump's Twitter, the platform for his communicational politics and the stage on which every day an institutional message containing critical topics for the government's agenda is deployed with the aid of a PowerPoint presentation. The aim is to break through the media to inform the people directly. In this regard, the current regime has developed an even more sophisticated communication platform than his predecessor, Enrique Peña Nieto. Peña Nieto used an army of bots to promote a favorable image of the president and his policies. In contrast, the daily mass media incendiarism ignited by the president's statements is being supported by a sophisticated structure on social media known as Red AMLO, with the purpose of disciplining and trolling critics of the president and his policies. The Mexican equivalent of *Time Magazine*, *Der Spiegel*, or *Le Nouvel Observateur*, political analysis magazine *Proceso* recently uncovered the Red AMLO network, which has the purpose of positioning certain key topics in public opinion through a combination of automatization and human intervention. There are indeed bots, but also real and monothematic Twitter and FB accounts that follow each other and create coordinated campaigns to shut the press down, disciplining journalists through harassment and hate speech. This form of inverted censorship is used also in China: anything critical published on the president is immediately stigmatized in the mass media and social networks. Bear in mind that Mexico is one of the most dangerous countries in the world to be a journalist, and that in the daily morning addresses, the president directly disqualifies prestigious journalists, publications and newspapers. A study by SPIN Taller de Comunicación Política (a workshop for political communication analysis founded in 2010) revealed that in 587 daily morning addresses given between December 2018 and April 2021, the president made 50,324 non-true affirmations.[1] The president's stand regarding the COVID-19 pandemic is that his religious amulets (escapularios) are protecting him, that it will all get better, and his government is doing a good job. At the other end of the day from the morning address is health secretary Hugo López Gatell's daily night address, who, with the aid of mathematic models and data, pedagogically describes the situation of the COVID-19 pandemic in Mexico. López Gatell has been lauded for his clarity, sharpness, articulateness, and for his infinite patience with dumb questions and for gladly and endlessly repeating himself for the sake of clarity. López Gatell's fantastic mathematics say it will all be over by the end of the summer, although he had forecasted the peak of contagion to be sometime in May, but that might never have happened. To me it is deeply troubling that the public/electorate is directly being fed data but without showing the peoples' ordeals. That has been the task of the international press: two videos were recently posted by *Al jazeera* and the *New York Times* showing troubling images of people being taken away to the hospital inside plastic cages in ambulances toward an uncertain destiny (hospitals are full full full, and apparently the app that determines which hospitals have beds for COVID-19 patients doesn't work properly). In the NYT video, a funeral home owner states that the death count in funeral homes exceeds by far the official count. We are not hearing stories—or at least they're being hidden by the president's shit storms and by López Gatell's data—of sick people dying or recovering, of small businesses shutting down or surviving, about networks of solidarity efforts, of abuse and survival, or presenting the points of view of nurses and doctors, the voices of children; what are taxi and Uber drivers, prostitutes, and owners of funeral homes and restaurants doing?

Coda

The passage of time materializes in unrecognizable fluctuations not due to organic change but to colonial devastation, industrial development, the construction of highways and roads, desiccation of rivers and lakes, deforestation, hydraulic presses, and five centuries of extractivism. Organic change is felt within inflamed bodies, vulnerable to disease, immune systems compromised by the toxicity surrounding us. We are not only seeing and feeling these fluctuations, but they also manifest in our bodies through epidemics of panic, anxiety, and autoimmune illnesses. Urban enclaves of privilege coexist with desolate landscapes of lost worlds and environmental devastation, and the sharp differences between privilege and destitution are the result of ignorance and denial of the responsibility we have as humans for looking after our relationships with other humans, our environment, the nonhuman.

The night before I finished this manuscript I had a nightmare that felt terrifyingly real: first, anguish for the loss of cell phone signal. Then the army declared curfew and picked up people from their homes to take them to a beautiful resort with lush gardens in which we all shared the torment of not having any news to read about the situation we were in from our cells. After many days of uncertainty, the group was split into men and women. Then we got uniforms to wear and were allotted to different working camps. All I could think of at that moment in the dream is that I wanted to write, to get my passport, my daughter, my partner, and my computer. The world as I knew it had ended arbitrarily and abruptly. It was already too late to run away, to change the future, to mourn the losses. I had this dream two months before the global COVID-19 pandemic changed the world forever in spite of collective denial and attempts to get things back to the "old normal."

In the face of incipient global authoritarianisms defending unsustainable structures of capitalist absolutism, struggles open up on various fronts: a deep rejection of heteropatriarchy, colonialism, white supremacy, and capitalism, which throughout these pages I have tried to articulate as a single movement. In order to dismantle heteropatriarchal structures, we need to break with collective alienation and begin to weave communities of resistance working together to alter the present and the future from the standpoint of love, generosity, persistence, engagement, and rebellion. In the world that we need to create there will be no room for authoritarian power, which is borne out of coercion and hierarchy. In that world, we will establish relationships based on reciprocity, respect, non-interference, freedom, and self-determination. Subjectivity will not be traversed by the false stigma of individuality or by gender mandates—gender will not even be an issue—and what will matter will be a search for a proper place and mission in the world and in one's community. There will also be consciousness that the land is what sustains life and that due to our lack of abilities and knowledges to ensure our own safety, survival, and prosperity, we need to make the market and market relationships disappear.[1] That is why we will have to learn from those who know how to survive without drainage systems, supermarkets, banks, and screens and understand that reciprocity, humility, honesty, and respect for others and the world, interdependence, are the means to assure the continuation of life on earth.

It is also necessary to reject the system from the standpoint of being aware that originary populations are occupied, erased, and displaced and that their bodies keep on being targets of colonial violence. The fact that Indigenous languages, forms of organization, culture, and folklore are celebrated, subsidized, exhibited, marketed, the subject of academic discussion, and part of the new official nationalism is a sign that originary populations are no longer perceived as a political and economic threat for the settlers.

If we posit the modern means of existing in the world as the main source of the problems we are currently facing, we can begin to recognize that existence does not derive from rational thinking but from emotional knowledge, from the movement of bodies across spaces, from what surrounds us, from what we feed ourselves with. That thought in itself is data produced in an isolated manner. Reason has become information whose power (above all, that of saving the future) is limited. Thinking is embodied, and the epidemics of autoimmune illnesses can be explained because we are in complete symbiosis with all systems that shape our consciousness and our capacities to learn, navigate, remember, interrelate. Unfortunately, these systems are toxic and polluted (with asbestos, plastic, GMOs, Netflix, hormones, mood altering substances). Our being in the world is not only "being-with" others but we also exist in our environment and depend on it to survive and thrive; that is why, when amplifying the sense of the I to encompass others and what surrounds us, we could understand that we exist symbiotically with what surrounds us. Therefore, we need to rethink life as a creative as opposed to productive act, based on self-determination beyond the market and relationships of production. For that, we need to create collective spaces where we can gather to think about how to organize and construct resistance and alternatives (like the feminist strike), with the consciousness of the need to transcend movements originated in indignation, trauma, or sadness.

Irmgard Emmelhainz
Mexico City, February 2021

Notes

INTRODUCTION

1.   All translations are my own, unless otherwise noted.

J'AI UNE VOIX DE CE QU'ON APPELLE "FEMME"

1.   Lauren Berlant, "The Book of Love is long and boring, no one can lift the damn thing . . ." *Berfrois* May 14, 2014, http://www.berfrois.com/2014/05/lauren-berlants-love-theory.
2.   Simone de Beauvoir, *The Second Sex*, trans. H. M. Parshley (New York: Vintage Books, 1989), 41.
3.   Ibid., 65.
4.   *I Will What I Want: Women, Design, and Empowerment*, co-curated by Jimena Acosta Romero and Michelle Millar Fisher. Its first venue was the Arnold and Sheila Aronson Galleries, at the Sheila C. Johnson Design Center (Parsons School of Design / The New School, New York) April 11–23, 2017. It then travelled to MUCA-Roma, in Mexico City, January 18 through May 22, 2018.
5.   Judith Butler, "Sex and Gender in Simone de Beauvoir's *Second Sex*" in "Simone de Beauvoir: Witness to a Century," special issue, *Yale French Studies*, no. 72 (1986), 36.
6.   Gayle Rubin, "The Traffic in Women: Notes on the 'Political Economy' of Sex," in *Toward an Anthropology of Women*, ed. Rayna Reiter (New York: Monthly Review Press, 1975), 162.

7.   Butler, "Sex and Gender," 37.

8.   Maggie Nelson, *The Argonauts*, (Minneapolis, MN: Greywolf Press, 2015), 12.

9.   Nelson, *The Argonauts*, 13.

10.   Nancy Fraser, "Contradictions of Capital and Care," *New Left Review*, no. 100 (July-August 2016), https://newleftreview.org/II/100/nancy-fraser-contradictions-of-capital-and-care.

11.   Fraser, "Contradictions of Capital and Care."

12.   Leila Slïmani, *Chanson douce* (Paris: Gallimard, 2016).

13.   Elizabeth Wilson, *Gut Feminism* (Durham, NC: Duke University Press, 2015).

14.   Beatriz Preciado (now Paul B. Preciado), *Testo Junkie: Sexo, drogas y biopolítica* (Madrid: Espasa, 2008).

REASONABLE MURDER

1.   Francoise Héritier, "L'Homme est la seule espèce dont les mâles tuent les femelles," *Sciences et avenir*, January 2012, https://www.sciencesetavenir.fr/fondamental/francoise-heritier-l-homme-est-la-seule-espece-dont-les-males-tuent-les-femelles_7660.

2.   D. E. Machina, "Letters to Chris Krauss: 'Kiss Me,' 'Fuck Me,' or 'Rape Me,'" libcom.org, March 28, 2011, https://libcom.org/forums/theory/letter-chris-kraus-'kiss-me'-'fuck-me'-or-'rape-me'-28032011.

A SENSORIUM OF VIOLENCE

1.   Sayak Valencia, *Gore Capitalism*, trans. John Pluecker (New York: Semiotext(e), 2018).

2.   See Walter Benjamin, "Critique of Violence," in *Reflections, Essays, Aphorisms, Autobiographical Writings*, trans. Edmund Jephcott (New York: Shocken Books, 1986); and Slavoj Zizek, *Violence* (New York: Picador, 2008).

3.   Frantz Fanon, *White Skins, Black Masks* (New York: Grove Press, 2008).

4.   Eimear McBride, *A Girl Is a Half-Formed Thing*, adapted for the stage by Annie Ryan (London: Faber and Faber, 2015), 56–57.

5.   Rita Segato, *Contra-pedagogías de la crueldad* (Buenos Aires: Prometeo, 2015).

LOVE REVOLUTION FEAR STRIKE

1.   "pero basta / para poner en marcha / todo esto." Alaíde Foppa, *Elogio de mi cuerpo* (México DF: Editorial Desconocida, 1970).

2.   Carlos Rangel, *Del buen salvaje al buen revolucionario* (Caracas: Monte Ávila Editores, 2009).

3. Yolanda Colom, *Mujeres en la alborada: Guerrilla y participación femenina en Guatemala 1973–1978* (Logroño: Pepitas de calabaza, 2018); and Aura Marina Arriola, *Este obstinado vivir* (La Antigua: Ediciones del pensativo, 2000).

4. For a beautiful portrait of Alaíde Foppa, see Elena Poniatowska, "Alaíde Foppa," *Debate feminista*, no. 2 (September 1990), https://debatefeminista. cieg.unam.mx/df_ojs/index.php/debate_feminista/article/view/1905.

5. This account of guerrilleras and their testimonies is by no means exhaustive.

6. Lourdes Uranga López, "Guerrilla y mujer: La construcción del hombre Nuevo o cómo cambiar el mundo sin cambiarlo," *La Jornada*, February 2, 2005, https://www.jornada.com.mx/2001/02/05/uranga_guer30.htm.

7. Lourdes Uranga López, *Comparezco y acuso* (México: Plaza y Janés, 2012).

8. Ingrid Betancourt, *Even Silence Has an End: My Six Years of Captivity* (New York: Penguin Press, 2010).

9. See Ingrid Betancourt, "What Six Years in Captivity Taught Me about Fear and Faith," TED2017, April 2017, https://www.ted.com/talks/ingrid_ betancourt_what_six_years_in_captivity_taught_me_about_fear_and_faith.

10. Laurence Debray, *Hija de revolucionarios* (Madrid: Anagrama, 2018), 47.

11. Debray, 48.

12. Diego Enrique Osorno, *El valiente ve la muerte solo una vez* (México D.F.: Era, 2020).

13. Martha Lamas, "Mujeres guerrerenses: Feminismo y política," *Revista Mexicana de Ciencias Políticas y Sociales*, 61, no. 226 (January–April 2016): 409–24.

14. See Verónica Gago, *La potencia feminista, o, El deseo de cambiarlo todo* (Madrid: Traficantes de sueños, 2019).

15. Gago, *La potencia feminista*, 28.

FROM LAS NIÑAS BIEN *TO THE* PRIMATES OF PARK AVENUE

1. Félix Guattari and Antonio Negri, *Les Nouveaux espaces de la liberté* (Paris: Éditions Lignes, 1985).

2. Guadalupe Amor, *Yo soy mi casa* (México DF: Fondo de Cultura Económica, 2018).

3. Wednesday Martin, *Primates of Park Avenue: A Memoir* (New York: Simon and Schuster, 2015).

4. Elena Poniatowska, *Fuerte es el silencio* (México DF: Era, 1980).

5. "Como Paquita, ahora libre, vive cerca del Palacio de Hierro, pensé "Qué bueno, porque así al salir, pasaré a la tienda a ver qué encuentro, una blusita, un fondito, unos calzoncitos, quizás una falda." [. . .] Ahora yo misma soy parte de la multitud que galopa hacia el Palacio de Hierro, de toda esta sociedad uniforme y fácilmente reconocible que piafa y cascabelea sobre los

pisos de madera, empujándose entre los mostradores, bufando, hurgando, buscando ¿qué?; soy el gran público que responde al anuncio Liquidación por inventario, Venta General, Ofertas Válidas del 22 al 26 de julio, rebaja de más de 30% en estos vestidos camiseros, tallas 12 a 22, modelos muy propios para la temporada de verano, en telas de fácil cuidado, Poliéster 100%, vienen con una manga corta, cuello sport y originales estampados en los colores de moda." Poniatowska, *Fuerte es el silencio*, 82.

6.   "Apagará la tele familiar y les hablará del socialismo a las ocho personas sentadas sobre la cama, ¿lo escucharían? ¿considerarían el cambio como un bien? ¿la libertad como un bien? ¿cuáles son para ellos los bienes de la vida? ¿acaso no son los bienes de consumo?" Poniatowska, *Fuerte es el silencio*, 82.

ONE ON ONE: LAKEVEREA VS. BELLAS ARTES

1.   See Susana Vargas, "Queer, Cuir y las sexualidades periféricas en México." *Horizontal* (December 15, 2016), https://hr.adigital.mx/queer-cuir-y-las-sexualidades-perifericas-en-mexico.

THE PREPROGRAMMED STATE OF BEING HAPPY

1.   Edgar Cabanas and Eva Illouz, *Manufacturing Happy Citizens: How the Science and Industry of Happiness Control Our Lives* (Cambridge, UK: Polity, 2019).

CRISIS OF RELATIONALITY AND BEING/HAVING

1.   Félix Guattari, *The Three Ecologies*, trans. Ian Pindar and Paul Sutton (New Brunswick, NJ: Athlone Press, 2000), 27.

2.   Franco "Bifo" Berardi, "Thatcher and Baudrillard," *Dr. Rinaldi's Horror Cabinet* (blog), September 4, 2017, https://socialecologies.wordpress.com/2017/09/04/franco-bifo-berardi-thatcher-and-baudrillard.

3.   Sarah Ahmed, *Living a Feminist Life* (Durham, NC: Duke University Press, 2017).

4.   Kathy Acker and McKenzie Wark, *I'm Very into You: Correspondence 1995–1996* (New York: Semiotext(e), 2015), 108.

5.   Leanne Simpson, *Islands of Decolonial Love* (Winnipeg: Arp Books, 2015), 103.

ABUSIVE LOVE

1.   Marta Lamas, *Acoso: ¿Denuncia legítima o victimización?* (México DF: FCE, 2018).

2. Marta Lamas, "El acoso y el #MeToo," *Revista de la universidad*, March 2019, https://www.revistadelauniversidad.mx/articles/c29fd42d-23ca-4e0e-a427-35170303a906/el-acoso-y-el-.

3. bell hooks, *All About Love: New Visions* (New York: William Morrow/Harper Collins, 2001).

4. Veronica Gonzalez, *The Sad Passions* (New York: Semiotext(e), 2013), 131–32.

AND WATER NOT RUNNING

1. Press Association, "Pro-Meat Protesters Fined for Eating Raw Squirrels at Vegan Stall," *Guardian*, July 23, 2019, https://www.theguardian.com/uk-news/2019/jul/23/pro-meat-protesters-fined-eating-raw-squirrels-vegan-stall.

2. "Le cayó un *me too*, como si esas cosas crecieran en los árboles y aterrizaran en el regazo de alguien, como fruta envenenada, la poesía es una cereza incómoda." Julián Herbert, "Ñoqui con entraña," *Ahora imagino cosas* (México: Literatura Random House, 2019), 93.

3. "El cuerpo femenino es una metonimia poderosa y que el precio que hay que pagar por eso es alto" Herbert, "Ñoqui con entraña," 97.

4. Vanessa Springora, *El consentimiento* (México: Lumen, 2020), 68.

VULNERABILITY

1. Arundhati Roy, *The Ministry of Utmost Happiness* (New York: Knopf, 2017), 442.

2. Nelson, *The Argonauts*, 101–2.

3. Jean-Luc Nancy, *Being Singular Plural* (Minneapolis, University of Minnesota Press, 2000).

4. Kim Turcot DiFruscia, "Shapes of Freedom: A Conversation with Elizabeth A. Povinelli, *e-flux Journal* #53 (March 2014), http://www.e-flux.com/journal/53/59889/shapes-of-freedom-a-conversation-with-elizabeth-a-povinelli.

5. Lauren Berlant, *Cruel Optimism* (Durham, NC: Duke University Press, 2011).

6. Leanne Simpson, *Islands of Decolonial Love* (Winnipeg: Arp Books, 2015), 103.

7. Carlos Rangel, *Del buen salvaje al buen revolucionario* (Caracas: Monte Ávila Ediciones, 2009), 331.

8. A reinterpretation of a fragment from Elizabeth Bishop's poem "The Map" (1934).

MORE ABOUT EMPATHY

1. Franco Berardi, *Breathing: Chaos and Poverty* (New York: Semiotext(e), 2018).

2. Susan Sontag, *Regarding the Pain of Others* (New York: Picador, 2003); Anita Chari, *A Political Economy of the Senses: Neoliberalism, Reification, Critique* (New York: Columbia University Press, 2015).

DECOLONIZATION

1. @YasnayaEG, "El amor romántico es al patriarcado lo que el nacionalismo es al estado," Twitter, Feb. 23, 2019, https://twitter.com/yasnayaeg/status/1099369271036182534; reprinted in Yásnaya Elena A. Gil, *Ää: Manifiestos sobre la diversidad lingüística*, compiled by Ana Aguilar Guevara, Julia Bravo Varela, Gustavo Ogarrio Bodillo, and Valentina Quaresma Rodríguez (México: Almadía, 2020), 45.
2. Roxanne Dunbar-Ortiz, "An Open Letter to President Barack Obama: Change the Columbus Holiday to Indigenous Peoples' Day," *Beacon Broadside*, October 9, 2014, https://www.beaconbroadside.com/broadside/2014/10/change-the-columbus-holiday.html.
3. Simpson, *Islands of Decolonial Love*, 45.
4. Gil, *Ää*, 27.
5. Nelson, *The Argonauts*, 101–2.
6. Nellie Bowels, "Human Contact Is Now a Luxury Good," *New York Times*, March 23, 2019, https://www.nytimes.com/2019/03/23/sunday-review/human-contact-luxury-screens.html.
7. Mandy Mayfield, "California Gov. Jerry Brown to Protesters during Climate Speech: 'Let's put you in the ground,'" *Washington Examiner*, November 11, 2017, http://www.washingtonexaminer.com/california-gov-jerry-brown-to-protesters-during-climate-speech-lets-put-you-in-the-ground/article/2640410.
8. Gil, *Ää*, 54.
9. Ibid.
10. "AMLO envía cartas a Felipe VI y al Papa Francisco: Pide se disculpen por abusos cometidos en la Conquista," *Proceso*, March 25, 2019, https://www.proceso.com.mx/nacional/2019/3/25/amlo-envia-cartas-felipe-vi-al-papa-francisco-pide-se-disculpen-por-abusos-cometidos-en-la-conquista-video-222231.html.
11. Angela Davis, Gayatri Chakravorty Spivak, and Nikita Dhawan, "Planetary Utopias," *Radical Philosophy*, no. 2.05 (Autumn 2019), https://www.radicalphilosophy.com/article/planetary-utopias.
12. Silvia Rivera Cusicanqui, *Un undo ch'ixi es posible: Ensayos desde un presente en crisis* (Buenos Aires: Tinta Limón, 2019).
13. "Y otra cosa, muy otra y más difícil, es ser mujer indígena zapatista. Entonces te decimos, hermana y compañera, que no les pedimos que vengan a luchar por nosotras, así como tampoco vamos a luchar por ustedes. Cada quien conoce su rumbo, su modo y su tiempo, su mundo." Sylvia

Marcos, "Un bosque de mujeres: Carta a las zapatistas" in *Tsunami 2*, ed. Gabriela Jáuregui (México DF: Sexto Piso, 2020), 145.

14. Eve Tuck and K. Wayne Yang, "Decolonization Is Not a Metaphor," *Decolonization: Indigeneity, Education & Society* 1, no. 1 (2012): 1–40.

15. Alain Badiou, *In Praise of Love*, trans. Peter Bush (New York: The New Press, 2012), 53.

16. Tuck and Yang, "Decolonization Is Not a Metaphor," 37.

17. Leanne Betamosake Simpson with Edna Manitowabi, "Theorizing Resurgence from within Nishnaabeg Thought," in *Centering Anishinaabeg Studies: Understanding the World through Stories*, eds. Jill Doerfler, Niigaanwewidam James Sinclair, Heidi Kiiwetinepinesiik Stark (Detroit: Michigan State University Press, 2013), 279–93.

MATERNITY SLAVERY REBELLION CREATIVITY JOUISSANCE

Dedicated to Lexie, Ruth, Margaret, Mos, Lulú, Pip, Marijose, Amy, Karla, Adriana, Gaby, Tats, Jimena, Lorena, Tatiana, and all the warrior-moms who are around and I admire.

1. Sian Cain, "Women Are Happier without Children or a Spouse," *Guardian*, May 25, 2019, https://www.theguardian.com/lifeandstyle/2019/may/25/women-happier-without-children-or-a-spouse-happiness-expert.

2. Lee Edelman, *No Future: Queer Theory and the Death Drive* (Durham, NC: Duke University Press, 2004).

3. Lina Meruane, *Contra los hijos* (México DF: Literatura Random House, 2018).

4. "Me he ido haciendo poco a poco, cuando me despierto por las noches a que me exprimas el pecho, la sal, la energía. Cuando lloro porque tu lloras. Cuando me voy de la habitación y te dejo llorar porque no sé como calmarte. También madrugadas como esta en que logré dormirte en mis brazos y yo aún sigo viva. [. . .] odio mi vida. mi cuerpo. mis mañanas. [. . .] de pronto tengo la sensación de qué mi vida es esto que no quería: disgustada por todo, todo el tiempo." Daniela Rea, "Mientras las niñas duermen," in *Tsunami*, ed. Gabriela Jáuregui (México DF: Sexto Piso, 2018), 48.

5. Adrienne Rich, *Of Woman Born: Motherhood as Experience and Institution* (New York: W.W. Norton, 1995).

VOICE DESIRE BODY DIFFERENCE LOVE

1. Marguerite Duras, *The Malady of Death* (New York: Grove Press, 1986), 27.

2. Georges Bataille, *Erotism, Death and Sensuality* (New York: Walker, 1962).

3. Denis de Rougemont, *Love in the Western World* (Princeton, NJ: Princeton University Press, 1982).

4. Maurice Blanchot, *The Inoperative Community* (Minneapolis: University of Minnesota Press, 1991).

EXISTENTIAL EROTICISM AND MODERNISM IN JEFF KOONS AND MARCEL DUCHAMP

1. André Breton, *Nadja* (New York: Grove Press, 1962)
2. "siempre que d recordaba a solas a su amiga la imaginaba así, extendida indolentemente sobre la cama, con las mantas que podían cubrirla invariablemente rechazadas aun cuando estaba dormitando, ofreciendo su cuerpo a la contemplación con un abandono total, como si el único motivo de su existencia fuese que d lo admirara y en realidad no le perteneciera a ella, sino a él y tal vez también a los mismos muebles del departamento y hasta a las inmóviles ramas de los árbol de la calle." Juan García Ponce, "El Gato," in *El gato y otros cuentos* (México DF: Fondo de Cultura Económica, 1984).
3. Octavio Paz, *La apariencia desnuda* (México DF: Era, 1973)
4. Byung-Chul Han, *La salvación de lo bello*, trans. Alberto Ciria (Madrid: Herder, 2015).
5. Preciado, *Testo Junkie*, 307.
6. Guadalupe Nettel, "Hongos," in *El matrimonio de los peces rojos* (Madrid: Editorial Páginas de Espuma, 2013), 83.
7. See Arwa Mahdawi, "Men Now Avoid Women at Work—Another Sign We're Being Punished for #MeToo," *Guardian*, August 29, 2019, https://www.theguardian.com/lifeandstyle/2019/aug/29/ men-women-workplace-study-harassment-harvard-metoo.

THE PENCIL OF NATURE AND OTHER APPROPRIATIONS

1. The masterclass is available online: Jill Soloway, "The Female Gaze: TIFF Master Class," Topple Productions, Sept. 11, 2016, https://www. toppleproductions.com/tiff-master-class-the-female-gaze.

NARCISSISM, HUMAN RIGHTS, AND POSTIMPERIALIST UTOPIAS

1. Alia Trabucco Zerán, *Las homicidas* (Madrid: Lumen 2019); and Susana Vargas Cervantes, *The Little Old Lady Killer: The Sensationalized Crimes of Mexico's First Female Serial Killer* (New York: New York University Press, 2019).
2. Angela Davis, Gayatri Chakravorty Spivak, and Nikita Dhawan, "Planetary Utopias," *Radical Philosophy*, no. 2.05 (Autumn 2019), https://www. radicalphilosophy.com/article/planetary-utopias.
3. Simone Weil, *The Need for Roots: Prelude to a Declaration of Duties towards Mankind*, trans. Arthur Wills (London: Routledge, 2002).

4. Dawn Marie Paley, *Guerra neoliberal: Desaparición y búsqueda en el norte de México* (México DF: Libertad Bajo Palabra, 2020).

5. Naomi Klein and Arundhati Roy, "A Global Green New Deal: Into the Portal, Leave No One Behind," Haymarket Books and Global Green New Deal, streamed live on May 19, 2020, https://www.youtube.com/watch?v=w0NY1_73mHY.

PALESTINE TODAY

1. Oliver Holmes, "A Jerusalem Hospital where Babies Die Alone," *Guardian*, June 20, 2019, https://www.theguardian.com/world/2019/jun/20/a-jerusalem-hospital-where-palestinian-babies-die-alone.

2. The Roadmap was an answer to the Second Intifada that had led to the escalation of violence and a wave of terrorist attacks ending in a massive Israeli military operation deployed in the West Bank known as Operation Defense Shield that resulted in Israeli military control over the West Bank.

3. The Flotilla sought to symbolically break the Gaza siege bringing humanitarian aid but was attacked by the IDF in international waters; nine people died in the attack, the rest of the crew and travelers were arrested, taken to Israel, and deported.

4. "Hitler Didn't Want to Exterminate the Jews," *Ha'aaretz*, October 21, 2015, https://www.haaretz.com/israel-news/netanyahu-absolves-hitler-of-guilt-1.5411578.

5. Netanyahu further tweeted on August 29, 2018: "The weak crumble, are slaughtered and are erased from history while the strong, for good or for ill, survive. The strong are respected, and alliances are made with the strong, and in the end peace is made with the strong"; @Israelipm, Twitter, Aug. 29, 2018, https://twitter.com/israelipm/status/1034849460344573952?lang=en.

6. David M. Halfbinger, "Netanyahu, Facing Tough Israel Election, Pledges to Annex a Third of the West Bank," *New York Times*, September 10, 2019, https://www.nytimes.com/2019/09/10/world/middleeast/netanyahu-israel-west-bank.html.

UPROOTING, RIGHTS, AND STATE VIOLENCE

1. Carlos Rangel, *Del buen salvaje al buen revolucionario: Mitos y realidades de América Latina* (Madrid: Gota a gota, 1976).

2. Cristina Rivera Garza, *La autobiografía del algodón* (México DF: Literatura Random House, 2020), 7.

3. Rivera Garza, *Autobiografía del algodón*, 7.

4. Simone Weil, *The Need for Roots* (London: Routledge, 2001), 37.

5. Elena Poniatowska, *Fuerte es el silencio* (México DF: Era, 1980), 64.

6. Paley, *Guerra neoliberal*.

TO DISMANTLE THE ENGINE

1.   Arundhati Roy, "Our Task Is to Disable the Engine," Progressive International, November 5, 2020, https://progressive.international/wire/2020-05-02-arundhati-roy-our-task-is-to-disable-the-engine/en.

2.   "Ecuador Sells a Third of its Amazon Rainforest to Chinese Oil Companies," *Business Insider*, March 28, 2013, https://www.businessinsider.com/ecuador-selling-its-rainforest-to-china-2013-3?r=MX&IR=T.

3.   Story, "Diarrhea, Dehydration, Hunger, Exhaustion": India's Rural Poor Suffer Most under Lockdown," Democracy Now, May 22, 2020, https://www.democracynow.org/2020/5/22/p_sainath_rural_india_coronavirus_neoliberal.

4.   Tom Philpot and Julia Lurie, "Here's the Real Problem with Almonds," *New Republic*, December 31, 2015, https://newrepublic.com/article/125450/heres-real-problem-almonds.

5.   Gabrielle Canon, "Watch Almonds Suck California Dry," *Mother Jones*, January 12, 2015, https://www.motherjones.com/media/2015/01/photos-matt-black-california-drought-almonds.

6.   Huiying Ng, "Soil's Metabolic Rift: Metabolizing Hope, Interrupting the Medium," *Technosphere Magazine*, May 29, 2019, https://technosphere-magazine.hkw.de/p/Soils-metabolic-rift-Metabolising-hope-interrupting-the-medium-8eMcSNrSza4JCGwpYsSEij.

7.   Naomi Klein, "The Screen New Deal," The Intercept, May 8, 2020, https://theintercept.com/2020/05/08/andrew-cuomo-eric-schmidt-coronavirus-tech-shock-doctrine.

8.   Guadalupe Fuentes López, "Antes que las eólicas, indígenas se quejaron de ser pisoteados. Y ellas, y gobiernos, los ignoraron," *Sin Embargo*, May 22, 2020, https://www.sinembargo.mx/22-05-2020/3789827.

9.   Gabriel Quadri De La Torre, "Termoeléctrica de Tula, el Chernóbil mexicano," *El Economista*, May 15, 2020, https://www.eleconomista.com.mx/opinion/Termoelectrica-de-Tula-el-Chernobil-mexicano-20200515-0020.html.

10.   Hermann Bellinghousen, "Frenar megaproyectos, exigen a López Obrador y a ocho gobernadores," *La Jornada*, May 24, 2020, https://www.jornada.com.mx/ultimas/politica/2020/05/24/frenar-megaproyectos-exigen-a-lopez-obrador-y-a-ocho-gobernadores-4894.html.

11.   Jodi Dean, "Neofeudalism and the End of Capitalism," *LA Review of Books*, May 12, 2020, https://lareviewofbooks.org/article/neofeudalism-the-end-of-capitalism.

THE NEW NORMALITY

1.   Eduardo Ruiz-Healy, "¿Cuáles de sus 'afirmaciones no verdaderas' se
     cree AMLO?," *El Economista*, April 27, 2021, https://www.eleconomista.
     com.mx/opinion/Cuales-de-sus-afirmaciones-no-verdaderas-se-cree-
     AMLO-20210427-0003.html.

CODA

1.   See Leanne Betasamosake Simpson, *As We Have Always Done: Indigenous
     Freedom through Radical Resistance* (Minneapolis: University of Minnesota
     Press, 2017); and Silvia Rivera Cusicanqui, *Un mundo ch'ixi es posible: En-
     sayos desde un presente en crisis* (Buenos Aires: Tinta Limón, 2018).

Index

www.ingramcontent.com/pod-product-compliance
Lightning Source LLC
Chambersburg PA
CBHW030332270326
41926CB00010B/1595